"David Meade has provided [...] Testament-focused missio[...] churches." "New Testament missionaries arose from a local church context. Missionary candidates weren't just volunteers jetting off on their own or independently joining a parachurch organization to forward their personal 'calling' apart from the local church. Qualified missionaries were sent by their local church, which commissioned them to go out." Bravo! David then leads readers through a broad and practical discussion of the local church, its' role in missions, the relations between churches and the missionaries they support, and between churches and missionary organizations. Sane, balanced, carefully biblical and always down to earth, he lays out the respective roles of sending churches, Pastors, congregations, missions teams, mission candidates and missionaries on the field.

As one who served as a missionary for some 33 years, I can testify that David touches upon many a sensitive and therefore neglected topic, challenging churches to be more than funding agencies; they should engage in actively shepherding those they send out, be involved in their labors and care for their welfare on an ongoing basis.

I recommend this book to every church, every Pastor, every member of a church's missions team and anyone considering missions. Missionary organizations leaders should likewise read this book and accommodate their labors to the principles laid out."

Rev. Baruch Maoz (MA)

"I have met people who know missions theology and others who know missions practices. I am thankful to know David Meade who knows both very well. Drawing from his experiences as a pioneer missionary, field leader, missions agency leader, local church elder, and church planter, David has given the readers an array of insights into biblical missions from multiple angles. It can be read straight through to gain a comprehensive perspective of church based missions as well as utilized as a field guide to get needed perspectives on specific missions questions. The story moving throughout the chapters of the book helpfully brings the theory into what it looks like in real church life. Highly recommended!"

John Crotts, Pastor of Faith Bible Church, Sharpsburg, GA

"The church has been God's plan A forever; no plan B exists." This sentence defines the essence of this long overdue book on the relationship between the local church and world missions. I've always believed what this book teaches and tried to practice it, but I would have done a much better job and avoided a lot of mistakes had this resource been available in my early years of pastoral ministry. It is essentially biblical, realistically practical, and it is refining our church's practice of missions. I hope it is distributed widely, read carefully, and implemented faithfully!

Mike DeVries, Pastor, Gateway Bible Fellowship

"First, it is hard to express how much I agree with the book, the case it is making, and the need to see the story of "Hopewell Church" spread to many more churches across America and beyond.

Part I of the book is wonderful; it is concise and practical, and its conclusion is inescapable. Part II. Chapters 8-15. Again, I really liked the chapters, and they are full of practical advice. I wish this book had existed 22 years ago when it could have helped my church send me. Part III: Chapters 16-23, we get to the nuts and bolts stuff here, and I love it. These pages contain lots of good practical advice, exhortation, and encouragement. I praise God for your work, David, and your experience, wisdom, and valuable ministry, which are there for all to see on nearly every page of the book."

Brian Wolf, Director of Missionary Training, MissioSERVE Alliance

"For far too many years, local churches have taken a backseat when it comes to the lives and ministries of the missionaries they send out. In Missions on Point, David Meade calls us back to a biblical vision of the local church at the center of missions—vetting, equipping, and sending her members to see God glorified among all nations."

Jay Decker, Director of Church Relations for Global Serve International

I have never seen such a comprehensive useable work on the subject. Every church leadership should devour then pass it to the troops. (Perhaps a syllabus could be put together for teaching the entire church for say 6 months of class time. It's that important.) I love the format. Especially the attendant Hopewell saga and how it reflects the teaching."

Jim Brown, church missions leader

Acts 13:1-3 describes an Antioch church focused on the Great Commission commands of Christ—and you and I have the Gospel today because of her obedience to them! This book pleads for churches in our time to become that kind of church and engage missions sending with the long view in mind. It provides helpful steps that church leaders can use as a pattern for getting the entire church involved in the blessings of missions sending. Mine the wisdom and experience offered, and become a local church whose vision includes unreached and unengaged peoples who have never heard there is a Jesus to believe in.

Denny Spitters, Church /Agency Coach 1615,
Co-Author of *When Everything Is Missions*

In *Missions on Point*, David Meade has provided a timely and practical "repatriation" to local churches of the privilege and responsibility of Christ's Great Commission. It is refreshing…Meade's book normalizes missions for "church" people, and normalizes the local church for "missions" people. It will assuredly help missions-hearted Christians engage unflinchingly in the life and purpose of the local church, and it will help local churches engage whole-heartedly in Christ's mission to get glory for Himself in the redemption of people from every nation, tongue, and tribe.

Smedly Yates, pastor at Grace Bible Church in Tempe, Arizona,
and board member of FinisTerre, a church-planting and
Bible-translation agency, helping churches plant churches in
the Finisterre Mountains of Papua New Guinea

This book is a goldmine of practical biblical step-by-step how to bring missions back to the oversight of the local church who have the goal of sending missionaries to unreached people groups for the purpose of seeing people saved and local churches set up and thriving for the glory of God.
I love this book. It is very practical. I learned a lot. I highly recommend it.

Martha Peace, MABC, Author of *The Excellent Wife*
and ACBC certified Biblical Counselor

David's qualifications for writing *Missions on Point* are extensive… I heartily endorse *Missions on Point* to both local churches and mission agencies. At minimum, it will cause you to scratch your theological head and think hard. Better yet, it may even cause a conceptual paradigm shift in the way you advocate doing missions.

Dr. Trevor A. Douglas, Grass-roots colleague of David working in the
Ifugao tribe, Philippines, Author of *Missionaries on Alert; Truth in Tension*

This book is a game-changer for anyone involved in or considering missions work, both for the sending church and the missionary. David's real-world expertise shines through on every page, making this a must-read… What sets this book apart is its biblical foundation, practical application, and inspiring case study of the "fictional" Hopewell Bible Church. This 'reality check' will resonate with anyone who has ever struggled to balance church-based missions with global outreach or vice versa. …I highly recommend this book to anyone seeking a Biblically sound path forward in their own mission endeavors.

My only wish? A workbook companion would be an amazing resource to help churches and missionary candidates apply these principles in their own lives and in their church.

Rick Wilson Managing Director, Entrusted Word Ministries

To have all the wisdom nuggets I've received from David in personal conversations and his podcast in one book, makes this resource invaluable! He is methodical, practical, and above all biblical. Everyone who reads David's book will find their missions trajectory sharpened:

For the prospective missionary, David writes, "Local churches in every ethnicity are the goal of missions (Matthew 28:18-20; Ephesians 3:20-21). You dare not neglect the role of the local church in your life and ministry." I wonder, do you believe this? David will guide you on a journey through Scripture that makes this abundantly clear.

For the sending church, David's book is a treasure trove for both pastoral leadership and the congregation who want to do the Great Commission right but need help with the first steps to take. A fruitful and practical way forward is possible!

And for the sending agency, we find both encouragement and rebuke to "find our lane" and stay in it for the Great Commission. We are reminded that we do not own the mission, but we do have the privilege to assist the church as it sends its church planters to the ends of the earth.

With David's help the missionary, the church, and the sending agency can all get on the same page of the Great Commission. And when that happens, the unreached will be reached for the sake of the Name of Jesus Christ!

Scott Maxwell, President, FinisTerre

MISSINS
ON POINT

*The Local Church at the
Heart of Ecclesiology
and Missiology*

DAVID C. MEADE

Scripture quotations are from the ESV® Bible (The Holy Bible, English Standard Version®), © 2001 by Crossway, a publishing ministry of Good News Publishers. Used by permission. All rights reserved.

Italics in Scripture quotations reflect the author's added emphasis.

Cover and interior formatting by KUHN Design Group | kuhndesigngroup.com

Copyright © 2024, David C. Meade

v.240723

All rights reserved. No part of this publication may be reproduced, stored in a retrieval system, or transmitted in any form or by any means—electronic, mechanical, photocopy, recording, or otherwise—without the prior written permission of the publisher, Send Forward. The only exception is brief quotations in published reviews.

ISBN 979-8-9883896-3-7 (Paperback)
ISBN 979-8-9883896-2-0 (Hardcover)

Send Forward
25 Willoughby Run
Sharpsburg, GA 30277

SendForward.org

*To all those fellow-warriors who faithfully
hold to the biblical and irreplaceable role
of the local church in world missions.*

CONTENTS

Preface 11
Introduction 13

PART 1: SEEING THE LOCAL CHURCH'S ROLE IN MISSIONS FROM THE WORD

Introduction to Part 1: Recognize Local Church
Missions Philosophy 21

1. The Local Church in Christ's View 29
2. The Local Church in Christ's Great Commission 45
3. The Local Church in Christ's Followers' Obedience 57
4. The Local Church in Christ's "All" of the New Testament ... 67
5. The Local Church in the Apostle Paul's View 79
6. The Local Church in God the Father's View 91
7. The Local Church in the Sending of Missionaries 101

PART 2: SECURING THE LOCAL CHURCH'S ROLE IN MISSIONS

Introduction to Part 2: Restore Local Church
Missions Philosophy 117

8. Satisfy Objections to Local Church Engagement
   in Missions 125
9. Sharpen the Biblical Goal of Missions 141
10. Select Missionaries from Your Midst 155
11. Search for a Strategic Missions Focus 169
12. Specify Your Church's Missions Resources 187
13. Stimulate Your Congregation for Missions Involvement 199

14. Sustain a Missions Culture in Your Church 211
15. Send and Shepherd Your Missionary Well 217

PART 3: SUSTAINING THE LOCAL CHURCH'S ROLE IN MISSIONS

Introduction to Part 3: Return to Local Church
Missions Partnerships 233
16. The Role of the Lead Pastor 239
17. The Role of the Missions Leader 247
18. The Role of the Missionary Mentor 255
19. The Role of the Missionary Candidate and Missionary 265
20. The Role of the Missions Agency 275
21. The Role of the Missions Donor 285
22. The Role of the Missionary-Training School 291
23. The Role of the Missions Mobilizer 297

Conclusion 305

APPENDICES

A. Why Is "Missions" Our Term of Choice? 311
B. What Are Good Resources for Church
Missions Development? 315
C. How Do We Choose a Missions Agency Partner? 323
D. Is My Church Too Small? 331

PREFACE

Nearly fifty years ago, I dreamed of parachuting into an unreached people group with just a backpack and a Bible. The big question in my mind was this: What kind of ministry should result there if I only used the Bible? The Lord gave me a burning desire to find the answer to that question in His Word. So, I read the New Testament, especially the Book of Acts, over and over again.

I became convinced by Scripture that planting local churches was the only reasonable answer to that one big question. I became a churchman. More than that, God used Scripture to show me that His big plan was to use local churches as His means to fulfill the Great Commission's mandate in every people group on earth. I became a missionary—a local-church-sent, local-church-planting missionary, to be exact.

The open secret revealed in the New Testament is the local church. Better stated, God's plan to display His wisdom and the glory of Christ in the gospel is to establish local churches everywhere. When you see a mystery revealed, you have an unexpected "aha" moment. With that understanding come humbling thoughts: "Why didn't I see that before? Why couldn't I have figured it out? It seems so simple now!" From that revelation onward, all the pieces fit together perfectly. You can't imagine how it remained such a mystery for so long. You see, on earth, worship alone is not the goal. Believers worshiping together in local churches is the goal.

This book focuses on biblical and practical foundations for the local church and missions. I hope the idea behind this book will explode in your imagination and ministry practice, as it did in mine. It might reshape how you think about the local church. I pray it will. The dynamics of the local church are enormous and extend well beyond the scope of world missions.

Now, I dare not proceed without giving thanks to the myriad of people God has used to make this book possible. The first is my wife, Kathy. She had no idea what she was getting when she said "Yes" and "I do" to marrying me. She has been the epitome of a beautiful, wise, gracious helpmate, teammate, spiritual companion, and encourager throughout our crazy-wild decades in God's providence, including a steady drumbeat of local-church-centric ministry.

Many others have shared in this book's plowing, seeding, watering, weeding, and nurturing. Their heartfelt yoke-fellowship has been vital to its production. Not least among those has been my intrepid assistant, Joel Hollins; the leaders and volunteers of Propempo International; the missions protagonists of Faith Bible Church; and a field of dear pastor friends who have prodded me to do this work. I thank God for every one of them.

Sharpsburg, GA
Soli Deo Gloria

INTRODUCTION

The thesis of this book is simple:

A. The Bible teaches that God has always planned to declare His wisdom and glory through local churches.

B. The New Testament shows local churches are the quintessential means in His design for Christ-centered gospel proclamation to every people group on earth.

C. All stakeholders in the global missions enterprise would be more effective if aligned in partnership with a local-church-oriented missions ministry philosophy.

The three parts of the thesis unfold in this way:

A. First, we'll consider biblical evidence showing that God has planned the Great Commission to be fulfilled through establishing local churches. Those churches then join the ongoing cycle of sending, going, and planting local churches.

B. Second, we'll propose how local churches can embrace and implement their role by applying seven practical principles.

C. Third, we'll consider how thoughtful implementation by every stakeholder in the missions-sending enterprise will build positive steps toward faithful partnership in this biblical local-church-centric mindset.

Dear reader, please allow the Scripture in this book to convince you of a local-church-centered philosophy of ministry. Don't skip over the Bible references, observations, and applications, though you might assume you've heard and seen them previously. I want you to look with wide-eyed wonder at something you've never seen, even though it was right in front of you.

This book turns a spotlight on the biblical role of the local church in world missions. (See appendix A for an explanation of why we use the term "missions.") It will awaken and challenge church leaders, missions leaders, missionaries, and everyone involved in the support and execution of missions to align with God's plan for His glory in and through the local church. Practical principles are offered for all the stakeholders and are supported by a thoughtful examination of biblical values and decades of experience in the missionary field, in cross-cultural missions leadership, and in pastoring within the local church.

Many churches and missions agencies have already experienced revolutionary positive impacts from the principles presented here. These truths have encouraged church leaders to step into their God-given roles in missions. Their churches have ignited with a more focused involvement in world missions. They have intentionally and joyfully raised up, trained, and sent their own to missions fields. Missionaries have become better qualified in every way for the challenging work of cross-cultural ministry as their churches send them out. Much to their surprise and delight, missions agencies have realized that those missionaries are the upper echelon of faithful and fruitful long-term workers among their ranks.

We who have long cherished this church-centered missions philosophy want to be crystal clear upfront that we sincerely appreciate missions agencies. For most of our decades of ministry, we have been a member of one or another agency. Missions agencies have an irreplaceable role in missions. We've long held that churches that wish to send out cross-cultural missionaries on their own both overestimate their capacity for, and underestimate the complexity of, doing so. Most churches that attempt this fail or at least regret their efforts. Thus, please do not view this book as favoring the local church to the exclusion of missions agencies. That is not the case! Local churches do need strong partner missions agencies to facilitate their and their missionaries' missions visions in the field.

Yet we must be honest: for too long, parachurch organizations have taken world missions captive. A few have no concern for local churches on either end of the spectrum: the sending side or the field side. Our dear brother organizations too often redefine missions however they choose without being challenged by the valid owner of the Great Commission, the church. Pragmatism reigns. Higher numerical outcomes become their guiding "Key Result Areas."

Even though most missions organizations were initially founded to serve local churches in their geographical, cultural, institutional, or technical specialty, they have typically become independent enterprises. They have a life of their own, which they unashamedly protect, promote, and propagate. They pray for and expect churches and donors to support the agency's ministry. They rarely have a vision for enabling and facilitating the missions ministries of local churches. Vision, field strategy, personnel management, and accountability are almost always initiated by and for the agency's benefit. Missions agencies can become self-perpetuating machines with little or no respect for the rightful role of the local church in missions. Yet a truly biblical vision for missions ministry is not just some imaginative goal for the agency's growth.

Local churches bear some culpability here. The local church has essentially given up its biblical role and responsibility to missions agencies (yes, even denominational entities). Local churches should reclaim their ownership. It's long past time for them to repatriate world missions into the sphere of the local church while seeking appropriate partnerships with sending agencies that can lend their particular expertise without dominating. This book aspires to provide a pathway to corrective change in this state of affairs.

If, by God's grace, we are successful in making our case, we hope it might start a tidal wave of change for the better in the entire missions enterprise. Churches will demand, with good reason, a place at the table. Missionary candidates will be better prepared and supported to do the work of missions ministry, having a more clearly focused end goal. Preventable attrition from the missions field will plummet. Missionary-sending churches and their missionaries will compel missions agencies to sign partnership agreements with the sending church. Donors will have a guide to help them be more discriminating in favor of supporting more local-church-centric ministries, more biblically focused goals, and better and longer-term results. Professors will not teach missions as a cold, historical progress of the gospel. Instead, they will lead their students to hearty engagement and maturing relationships with healthy sending churches.

How can this be accomplished? We start with incontrovertible biblical evidence for the centrality of the local church in God's plan for

His glory and the fulfillment of the Great Commission. Then, in practical terms, we learn how these principles work in our local churches and missions today. These biblical, theological, and practical lenses will frame a fresh vision of the role of each party in the work of missions. I'll suggest commitments for the stakeholders that, Lord willing, will make it all fit together seamlessly for effective implementation.

The book will include some anecdotes about churches we've helped to become aligned with local-church-centric missions. In particular, we've created a composite serial narrative of a church progressively awakening to these principles and applying them; the narrative is based on real-life situations but is anonymized for privacy and security purposes. Lastly, several appendices provide practical references and solutions to help you with implementation in your respective role(s).

PART 1

SEEING THE LOCAL CHURCH'S ROLE IN MISSIONS FROM THE WORD

INTRODUCTION TO PART 1

RECOGNIZE LOCAL CHURCH MISSIONS PHILOSOPHY

Though I am a missionary, if you cut me, I bleed local church. We will see in part 1 that the local church is foundational to understanding the New Testament. When using the Bible to point this out to church leaders, we see remarkable responses from pastors. The key is the local church's role as both the beginning and the end of world missions. The pastors in the audience immediately perceive other practical implications as well. One pastor with multiple graduate degrees from renowned seminaries literally slapped his head, exclaiming, "I got it!" Another one melted in tears. Yet others have confessed, "They never taught us this in seminary."

Pastors are an easy audience to convince that the local church is essential. After all, it is their livelihood! They've committed years of preparation and tireless ministry in public, in private, and in their studies to the local body of Christ. "Of course, the local church is important, even central, to the message of the New Testament," they say. But somehow, the content presented in this book strikes them as fresh and revolutionary. So, let's start at the beginning.

Part 1 of this book is about biblical ecclesiology, particularly with respect to missions. We'll primarily consider the biblical and practical foundations of the local church and missions. May God use it to reshape your understanding and change how you think about missions and the local church.

HOW THE WORD "CHURCH" IS USED

Briefly consider an overview of the term "church," or *ekklesia*, in the New Testament. There are 109 references to "church" in the New Testament. The word is predominantly applied to a local assembly of believers—i.e., a local church.

The plural usage refers to a group of local churches in a region:

- "the churches of Galatia/Judea" (Galatians 1:2, 22; 1 Corinthians 16:1, 19; 1 Thessalonians 2:14; Revelation 1:4, 11, 20)
- or a number of churches, as in "churches" or "other churches" (Acts 15:41; 16:5; 2 Corinthians 11:8)
- or all local churches together, as in "all the churches" or "churches" in general (Romans 16:4, 16; 1 Corinthians 7:17; 14:33; 2 Corinthians 8:1, 18, 23–24; 11:8, 28; 12:13; 2 Thessalonians 1:4; Revelation 2:7, 11, 17, 23, 29; 3:6, 13, 22; 22:16)

IMAGES OF THE CHURCH IN THE NEW TESTAMENT

It's also helpful to recall how the church is referred to in images or analogies in the New Testament. The church is referred to as:

- a family
- the bride of Christ

- a new temple or God's house
- a holy priesthood
- the pillar and bulwark of truth
- the body of Christ

Note that all of these have as their basis interdependent relationships, mutuality, a special relationship to God and His truth, and a particular relationship to Christ.

INVISIBLE CHURCH VS. VISIBLE CHURCH

The terms "universal church" and "invisible church" are usually intended to mean the collection of all believers, regardless of location or even time. The terms "visible church" and "local church" are intended to mean the collection of mutually committed believers in a particular location: a local church, or perhaps a group of local churches. The New Testament primarily refers to local churches using the term "church," or *ekklesia*. In fact, as a general rule, the default interpretation of the term "church" as used in the New Testament should be understood as referring to a local church or a group of local churches. Only when the term "church" is used in a context for which local church does not make sense should it be interpreted as the universal church.

Robert Saucy writes, "As for membership in an invisible church without fellowship with any local assembly, this concept is never contemplated in the New Testament. The universal church was the universal fellowship of believers who met visibly in local assemblies."[1]

John MacArthur states is this way: "There is no such thing as a believer in the New Testament who exists in some kind of random,

---
1. Robert Saucy, *The Church in God's Program* (Chicago: Moody Press, 1972), 17.

independent, free-floating kind of lifestyle. All believers were collected into local assemblies."[2]

THE LOCAL CHURCH IS ESSENTIAL TO EVERY BELIEVER

From Acts 2 onward, the New Testament exhibits and assumes that every believer will be a vital, active member of a local assembly. There is no room for believers to be church hoppers. There is no allowance for lone-ranger Christians. One test to prove the assertion may suffice: How can a nonaffiliated, uninvolved professing believer obey the forty-plus "one another" commands of the New Testament apart from frequent face-to-face relationships with a mutually committed body of believers?

As we survey the teaching of the New Testament, we will see through the macro context of the life of the church and books of the New Testament that the local church was and is the default understanding of the context of Christian life, including fellowship, growth, accountability, and obedience to the Lord's commands.

WALKING THROUGH THE BIBLICAL EVIDENCE

Part 1 will introduce you to the core concept of the biblical centrality of the local church from seven related perspectives. Here's a high-altitude overview.

In looking at "Christ's View," we'll consider the Lord Jesus Christ's instruction to local churches, His relationship with and love of the

---

2. John MacArthur, "Why You Should Join the Church," Grace to You, January 27, 2008, https://www.gty.org/library/sermons-library/80-330/why-you-should-join-the-church.

church, and His concern for the well-being of the church, especially local churches.

In considering "Christ's Great Commission," we'll see how the Great Commission, as expressed in Matthew 28, cannot be fulfilled apart from planting indigenous local churches. Local churches are the desired result of Great Commission ministry. Other expressions of the Great Commission bolster this conclusion.

Turning to "Christ's Followers' Obedience," building on the above insight into the Great Commission, we find that the original hearers of Jesus' Great Commission understood, owned, and acted upon this conclusion. The firsthand and secondhand hearers obeyed the mandate by planting churches through the power of the gospel, the Word, and the Holy Spirit.

In explaining "Christ's 'All' of the New Testament," we note how, as part of the Great Commission, our Lord's instructions included "teaching them to observe all that I have commanded you." We understand that "all" to be the entire New Testament. The inspiration of the New Testament and its composition in itself is confirming testimony to the centrality of the local church in God's program, including missions.

In considering the "Apostle Paul's View," we realize that a comprehensive study of the Apostle Paul in regard to the church and its centrality in world missions is a larger task than this book can undertake. We can, however, make some key observations that again build the case for the local church's role in world missions.

In our look at "God the Father's View," we recognize that it is a good thing to take a step back and see the big picture, as expressed in Scripture, from God's point of view. Doing so will reinforce and encourage us in this line of thought.

Moving on to the "Sending of Missionaries," we observe how the

New Testament word *propempo* develops the concept of "sending forward" in a specialized missionary capacity. Over the course of time, in the inspired New Testament, *propempo* became a shorthand term for the local church sending out missionaries to the unreached for gospel, church-planting, and church-strengthening ministries.

SO WHAT? WHAT DIFFERENCE DOES IT MAKE?

Understanding this biblical perspective on the local church fuels and confirms our intuitive suspicions that the local church is vital to world missions! It moves the needle in our calibration from "I thought the local church was supposed to be significant; I always thought it was key to God's work" to "Now I know for sure." This concept, Lord willing, will become a factor for positive change in the enterprise of world missions.

A church in Ohio got it. They thought they were a great missions-minded church. They gave a lot of money to missions. They had an annual missions conference. Yet it slowly dawned on them that, in reality, they were little more than a paymaster for more missionaries than was healthy. Hard financial times hit. They called for help.

Starting at the beginning—from the Bible—the church's leaders and Missions Team awakened to their larger role and responsibility for world missions in and through their congregation. They also learned better practices and built a plan to restore focus and ownership to their missions relationships. Now, the whole congregation is excited about their role in missions. They have well-defined values that serve as guardrails for their decisions and commitments. They are actively raising up and sending their own members into missions. They confidently embrace and see the fruit of making their local church the center point of their world missions.

Implementing a more biblical role for the local church in world missions fundamentally improves how we do missions. It will:

- give greater confidence to the pastor and other leaders as they guide their church in missions
- produce broader and stronger congregational involvement in missions
- raise up better-qualified long-term missionaries for the push toward seeing the Great Commission fulfilled with a healthy church planted in every people group
- focus joint training with institutions on a more robust balance of character, convictions, and competence for cross-cultural workers
- shepherd and support missionaries in every way, enabling them to survive and thrive in field ministry life in those remaining hard places
- give missions agencies better outcomes in every respect in the field and lessen their burden in "member care"
- result in more healthy churches planted in the people groups of the world to further the completion of the Great Commission mandate

By God's grace, may it be so!

THE LOCAL CHURCH IN CHRIST'S VIEW

Matthew 16:13–21 reads:

> Now when Jesus came into the district of Caesarea Philippi, he asked his disciples, "Who do people say that the Son of Man is?" And they said, "Some say John the Baptist, others say Elijah, and others Jeremiah or one of the prophets." He said to them, "But who do you say that I am?" Simon Peter replied, "You are the Christ, the Son of the living God." And Jesus answered him, "Blessed are you, Simon Bar-Jonah! For flesh and blood has not revealed this to you, but my Father who is in heaven. And I tell you, you are Peter, and on this rock I will build my church, and the gates of hell shall not prevail against it. I will give you the keys of the kingdom of heaven, and whatever you bind on earth shall be bound in heaven, and whatever you loose on earth shall be loosed in heaven." Then he strictly charged the disciples to tell no one that he was the Christ.

> From that time Jesus began to show his disciples that he must go to Jerusalem and suffer many things from the elders and chief priests and scribes, and be killed, and on the third day be raised.

Look at this passage in context and notice Christ's use of the word "church." Two observations quickly occur. One is that we know that the "rock" on which Jesus builds His church is not Peter. This is a play on words. "Peter" means a piece of rock or a stone. The "rock" of verse 18 is a mass of rock or large stone. The rest of the New Testament gives no indication that Peter himself was the foundation.

Instead, the statement or confession with which Peter answered Jesus shows that Jesus is the rock on which the church is built, and this is confirmed for us in 1 John several times, notably in 1 John 5:1, which states, "Everyone who believes that Jesus is the Christ has been born of God, and everyone who loves the Father loves whoever has been born of him."

John's statement is an echo of the confession that Jesus is Lord. He is the Messiah. I love this quote from a dear pastor friend, Donny Martin: "Jesus has only one building project, and it is the church."

CHRIST TEACHES ON LOCAL CHURCH PURITY AND AUTHORITY

The next time Christ uses the term "church" is in Matthew 18. The context is a set of engaging interactions with people about temptation and about being lost and found. Jesus says this in Matthew 18:15–20:

> If your brother sins against you, go and tell him his fault, between you and him alone. If he listens to you, you have gained your brother. But if he does not listen, take one

or two others along with you, that every charge may be established by the evidence of two or three witnesses. If he refuses to listen to them, tell it to the church. And if he refuses to listen even to the church, let him be to you as a Gentile and a tax collector. Truly, I say to you, whatever you bind on earth shall be bound in heaven, and whatever you loose on earth shall be loosed in heaven. Again I say to you, if two of you agree on earth about anything they ask, it will be done for them by my Father in heaven. For where two or three are gathered in my name, there am I among them.

There are so many connections in this passage to the local church. This passage is Christ's instruction on church purity and restoration, sometimes called church discipline. It's very clear that the teaching must be applied within local churches. He outlines our local church relationships and accountability to each other when a brother is in a pattern of unrepentant sin. The steps or stages of church discipline do not make sense when applied to the universal church. The goal is restoration. He instructs about the interpersonal interaction and the process of restoring the erring brother to fellowship again. Christ's example also shows that the local church has the authority to discipline and to restore. Note the parallelism between what He tells Peter about binding and loosing in Matthew 16:19 and what He says here in Matthew 18:18–20.

It is evident in this context that Jesus is teaching about the local church. How much grief would be spared and how much restoration would be affected by following Christ's guidance! His instruction shows that He knows local churches will have problems with gossip, accusations, conflict, immorality, clearly sinful behavior, and lack of repentance. Local church ministry is messy human stuff! Christians following these steps learn to discern and get objective confirmation of the damaging insinuations or potentially sinful patterns. First, go to the offender privately. Then go semi-privately. Involve church leaders' counsel. Finally, go public. How quickly gossip would be extinguished if we followed this course! So many misinterpretations and biased judgments might be eliminated at the source. Sinners would be brought to face their errant choices and the consequences of an unrepentant attitude.

CHRIST PROTECTS AND DEFENDS HIS CHURCH

Now, let's proceed to Acts 9, where Jesus makes a surprise appearance. Saul, who later became known as Paul, was persecuting the church. He was going after believers and had permission from the Jewish authorities to persecute Christians. On his way to Damascus, a light from heaven flashed around him. Acts 9:1–6 reads:

> But Saul, still breathing threats and murder against the disciples of the Lord, went to the high priest and asked him for letters to the synagogues at Damascus, so that if he found any belonging to the Way, men or women, he might bring them bound to Jerusalem. Now as he went on his way, he approached Damascus, and suddenly a light from heaven shone around him. And falling to the ground, he heard a voice saying to him, "Saul, Saul, why are you persecuting me?" And he said, "Who are you, Lord?" And he said, "I am Jesus, whom you are

persecuting. But rise and enter the city, and you will be told what you are to do."

You must not lose the importance of this story in Luke's chronicle. Saul is going to persecute Christians in a particular place: Damascus. Jesus says to Saul, "You are persecuting Me." Jesus identifies so personally with a local group of believers in Damascus that as Paul persecuted them, Paul was persecuting Christ Himself. This certainly points to the significance of the local church in the mind of Christ.

We can go back to make the connection with the account of Paul's persecution of the church from Acts 8:1–3:

> And Saul approved of his [Stephen's] execution.
>
> And there arose on that day a great persecution against the church in Jerusalem, and they were all scattered throughout the regions of Judea and Samaria, except the apostles. Devout men buried Stephen and made great lamentation over him. But Saul was ravaging *the church*, and entering house after house, he dragged off men and women and committed them to prison.

The question is: Do Acts 8 and 9 refer to the universal church in general or to specific local churches? While it would be easy to make these passages apply to the universal church in general, the greater context of Acts 8 and 9 shows the description of disciples within a particular locality.

- 8:1: The church in Jerusalem was persecuted.
- 8:1: The disciples were scattered to Judea and Samaria.

- 8:3: Saul was "ravaging the church" in particular localities.

- 9:2ff: Paul obtained specific permission to persecute the disciples connected to synagogues in particular localities of Damascus. If the synagogues were local synagogues, then the church or churches of Damascus were local churches. Undoubtedly, disciples of the local church in Damascus—not some faceless universal church—helped Paul escape threats to his life.

CHRIST LOVES THE CHURCH

Now, let's look at Ephesians 5. We will look at Ephesians 5 again when we talk about Paul. However, as we consider Christ's view of the church, we must study Ephesians 5:22–33:

> Wives, submit to your own husbands, as to the Lord. For the husband is the head of the wife even as Christ is the head of the church, his body, and is himself its Savior. Now as the church submits to Christ, so also wives should submit in everything to their husbands.
>
> Husbands, love your wives, as Christ loved the church and gave himself up for her, that he might sanctify her, having cleansed her by the washing of water with the word, so that he might present the church to himself in splendor, without spot or wrinkle or any such thing, that she might be holy and without blemish. In the same way husbands should love their wives as their own bodies. He who loves his wife loves himself. For no one ever hated his own flesh, but nourishes and cherishes it, just

as Christ does the church, because we are members of his body. "Therefore a man shall leave his father and mother and hold fast to his wife, and the two shall become one flesh." This mystery is profound, and I am saying that it refers to Christ and the church. However, let each one of you love his wife as himself, and let the wife see that she respects her husband.

Though this passage is not a record of Christ speaking directly about the church, it is inspired by the Holy Spirit through Paul to speak of Christ's relationship to the church. It is the most densely packed set of references to the church in the Bible. Six times, the word "church" is used directly. Seven times, the church is mentioned in this passage as "his body" (two times), "its," "her" (three times), or "she."

Christ values the church so much that He gave Himself for her. He does everything for her so that He might present her to Himself in splendor, holy and without blemish. Notably, the term for "love" throughout this passage is *agape*, the self-sacrificing, unconditional love for the good of another.

It makes sense to take the references for the church here to be primarily about Christ's love for the universal church. However, the focused relationship and intimacy described also make sense when applied to local churches. In a way, part of the profound mystery may be that Christ can have that kind of singular relationship described here with the church at large and yet have the same love and care for all local churches everywhere simultaneously without contradiction or diminution of quality. We can say, "Christ loves my church. He desires to present us, our local body with all our foibles, to Himself as holy and without blemish."

CHRIST ORIGINATED TEACHING ON THE ADMINISTRATION OF LOCAL CHURCHES

According to Paul's testimony throughout his ministry, the Lord Jesus Christ Himself taught Paul the essentials of local church body life and leadership. We italicize some phrases here to emphasize this claim.

> Acts 22:14–15: "And he [Ananias] said, 'The God of our fathers appointed you to know his will, to *see the Righteous One and to hear a voice from his mouth*; for you will be a witness for him to everyone of what you have seen and heard.'"

> Romans 12:3–5: "For *by the grace given to me* I say to everyone among you not to think of himself more highly than he ought to think, but to think with sober judgment, each according to the measure of faith that God has assigned. For as in one body we have many members, and the members do not all have the same function, so we, though many, are one body in Christ, and individually members one of another."

> 1 Corinthians 11:23: "For *I received from the Lord* what I also delivered to you, that the Lord Jesus on the night when he was betrayed…"

> 1 Corinthians 14:37: "If anyone thinks that he is a prophet, or spiritual, he should acknowledge that *the things I am writing to you are a command of the Lord.*"

> 1 Corinthians 15:3: "For I delivered to you as of first importance *what I also received*: that Christ died for our sins in accordance with the Scriptures,

Galatians 1:1: "Not from men nor through man, but *through Jesus Christ* and God the Father…"

Galatians 1:15–18: "But when he who had set me apart before I was born, and who called me by his grace, was pleased to reveal his Son to me, in order that I might preach him among the Gentiles, *I did not immediately consult with anyone*; nor did I go up to Jerusalem to those who were apostles before me, *but I went away into Arabia*, and returned again to Damascus. Then after three years I went up to Jerusalem."

Ephesians 3:1–3: "For this reason I, Paul, a prisoner of Christ Jesus on behalf of you Gentiles—assuming that you have heard of *the stewardship of God's grace that was given to me for you, how the mystery was made known to me by revelation*, as I have written briefly."

Ephesians 3:8–10: "To me, though I am the very least of all the saints, this grace was given, to preach to the Gentiles the unsearchable riches of Christ, *and to bring to light for everyone what is the plan of the mystery* hidden for ages in God, who created all things, *so that through the church the manifold wisdom of God might now be made known*."

1 Timothy 6:3: "If anyone teaches a different doctrine and does not agree with *the sound words of our Lord Jesus Christ* and the teaching that accords with godliness…"

This teaching about the local church was a priority to Christ. Thus, it likewise became Paul's priority throughout his apostolic ministry.

Everywhere Paul went, he established local churches, appointed and taught church leaders, and passed on his tutelage from Christ about essentials such as the order and dynamic relationships within the local church, the forty-plus "one anothers," the exercise of gifts, and the church ordinances of baptism and the Lord's Supper, as well as the offices and roles of local church leaders and servants.

Paul received his special revelation about the nature of the operation of local churches from Christ (referred to in Ephesians 3:9 as "the plan [or, in some versions, "the administration"] of the mystery"). We believe that during the approximately three years Paul spent in "Arabia," there was a time of individual study, contemplation, and intense, personal special revelation from Christ regarding all aspects of Paul's future ministry. That training was not just about the gospel, as highlighted in Galatians, but included everything about the local church's household administration and exercise of body life.[3]

Paul reinforces his special revelation from Christ and, therefore, His authority in several ways in the epistles. One is by using the word *entrusted* concerning himself and his charge to accurately communicate the message of Christ and His church (see 1 Corinthians 9:17; Galatians 2:7; 1 Thessalonians 2:4; 1 Timothy 1:11; 2 Timothy 1:12; Titus 1:3). He knew that he had been given a special trust as an Apostle of Jesus Christ by Christ Himself. Paul was determined to fulfill that trust faithfully.

---

3. See A. T. Robertson's argument as an example. Archibald Thomas Robertson, *Word Pictures in the New Testament*, Volume IV, *The Epistles of Paul* (Grand Rapids: Baker Book House, 1931), 278–281.

CHRIST'S SPECIAL CARE FOR LOCAL CHURCHES IN THE END

Somehow, we often fail to recognize the focused attention and care of Jesus Christ for local churches in the last book of the Bible, Revelation. The Apostle John gives the setting for Revelation, addressing it to "the seven churches that are in Asia" (Revelation 1:4).

In Revelation 1:19–20, Christ charges John to write what he sees in this inspired book:

> Write therefore the things that you have seen, those that are and those that are to take place after this. As for the mystery of the seven stars that you saw in my right hand, and the seven golden lampstands, the seven stars are the angels of the seven churches, and the seven lampstands are the seven churches.

In the first three chapters, Jesus is passing along commendation, corrective instruction, and compassion through John to the seven churches of Asia. Almost sixty years after His ascension, Jesus appeared to John to give instructions about unique issues and current events in local churches around the area where John lived and ministered.

These were specific local churches. The single big-picture concept I want you to grasp is that Christ knew each of those churches intimately. He knew explicit details about them. He knew the motives and aspirations of the individual members of each church. He knew the names of their leaders. He knew the names of sinful offenders within the church. He communicated corrections appropriate for each church. He urged them to follow His instruction. Christ makes it very clear that He has local churches on His heart—specific local churches—and He knows everything about them very well.

But wait, there's more! We don't get to the end of the Book of Revelation until chapter 22. Between the first three chapters of the book and the last two chapters, there is a lot of revelation and eschatological imagery: angels, scenes in heaven, scenes on earth, scenes under the earth, destruction, martyrdom, worship, death, and judgment. Revelation is filled with apocalyptic and enigmatic symbols. Then, in Revelation 21, we see the new heaven and new earth. We see God on the throne and glorious in specific scenes of the New Jerusalem. Then Jesus says this in Revelation 22:16: "I, Jesus, have sent my angel to testify to you about these things for the churches. I am the root and the descendant of David, the bright morning star."

Jesus tells John that the revelation he has seen and is recording is "for the churches." Because of the plural usage, there is no question about whether this is about local churches or the universal church. The universal church is made up of local churches everywhere. But Jesus is more specific here. He tells John that this revelation is for the sake of local churches everywhere. Be ready, churches! Be holy, bride of Christ! Be hope-filled! Jesus wins!

From Matthew to Revelation, the New Testament is sprinkled with Christ's love and care for local churches. He is aware of the sinful proclivities of the real people who comprise those congregations. Still, local churches are a part of His design as the fruit of the gospel. An expression of supernatural fellowship among a diverse, mutually committed body of believers, they display His wisdom and glory to the world.

At this point, you may be wondering how we got this far without addressing the Great Commission of Jesus Christ. Dear reader, that is coming in the next chapter.

INTRODUCING HOPEWELL BIBLE CHURCH

Hopewell Bible Church is a composite of a typical church that has been helped in understanding and applying the message of this book. Throughout the book, this story will unfold and enable you to see, in part, how a biblical local-church missions philosophy works out. It's a serialized story based on factual experiences from several real churches. The names are all made up. Although the details of the story shouldn't be tied too closely to specific people and situations, the goal is to portray people and issues realistically. The story focuses on one church's development, sending, and shepherding of a married couple. (Please know, though, that singles are also valuable teammates on church planting teams and related ministries.) I'll give you a bit of the story at the close of each chapter.

Hopewell Bible Church (also referred to as "HBC" or "Hopewell") is in the middle of somewhere, within an hour of some major city. It is one hundred years old at the start of our story. Hopewell owns its property outright and has no outstanding debt. The property and facilities have room for growth. Its facilities always have some repair or renovation projects, year by year.

The average Sunday morning attendance is about 350 people. It is a diverse group—ethnically, economically, and vocationally—with some multigenerational extended families well represented in the church's life. The attendance has been steady for the past twenty years, with Hopewell losing about as many as it gains through all of the area's economic, industrial, and political ups and downs, as well as through natural attrition and addition.

Hopewell operates with a modified congregational polity. It has a plurality of elders: six men, including the senior pastor. The elders' ages span forty years between the oldest and youngest. Hopewell also has ten people designated as deacons serving the church in their respective areas of ministry. The senior pastor, Aaron Blake, has been there for twenty years. He is well respected in the church and community. He is known as a solid Bible teacher and a mature, godly leader of the church. Hopewell is also known as a healthy, Bible-oriented church, clearly proclaiming the gospel, teaching the Word, caring well for its members, and loving missions. The church supports a dozen missionaries and missions ministries with modest regular financial partnerships.

A CRITICAL TURNING POINT ARISES

One Sunday morning, Pastor Aaron Blake stood in his typical "greet the congregation" location after the service. Among the steady stream of congregants, a man and a woman approached him with serious faces. Pastor Aaron quickly racked his brain as his hand raised to meet theirs in a handshake. He heaved an internal sigh of relief; he remembered them!

Kevin and Melissa Langford had been members at Hopewell for less than a year. They were a young married couple with no children. They moved to the area because Kevin got an excellent job, compatible with his university degree, at a manufacturing plant nearby. They seemed earnest enough. Pastor Aaron remembered that the Langfords had diligently looked for a church. They chose Hopewell because of its sound Bible teaching and history of interest in world missions.

Kevin shook Pastor Aaron's hand, thanked him for the morning message, and said, "Pastor, we'd like you to know that we believe God is calling us into missions. We'd like Hopewell, our home church, to help us go to the field."

Inside his head, Pastor Aaron thought, "Wait, what did you say? OK. Don't show panic. Don't show panic."

What he actually said was: "Wow, that's great! Yes, we'll have to talk about that."

Then he thought, "OK. Now panic."

THE LOCAL CHURCH IN CHRIST'S GREAT COMMISSION

Even missions-minded Christian communities often misunderstand and sometimes even misrepresent the Great Commission. A lot of churchgoers think that the Great Commission is only one passage in the Bible. Or they believe the Great Commission is just a collection of a few passages from the Gospels. However, the basis for the Great Commission is present throughout the Scriptures, from Genesis to Revelation.

Another popular misconception is that the Great Commission is exclusively about going to the nations and evangelizing. Period. However, as we will see, the Great Commission is much deeper, richer, and fuller than that.

Obedience to Christ's Great Commission mandate anticipates a particular result. Let's look at this cluster of similar commands in the Gospels and the Book of Acts. We'll start in Mark, work through the Gospels and Acts, and return to Matthew.

THE GREAT COMMISSION IN MARK

Mark 16:15 reads, "And he said to them, 'Go into all the world and proclaim the gospel to the whole creation.'"

This verse is the version of the Great Commission recorded in the Gospel of Mark. It is consistent with Jesus' teaching throughout His ministry. It also has a few elements that we will see in the other instances. "Go" is used to mean going out, presumably from wherever you live into all the world. It is comprehensive in its scope. "Proclaim the gospel" is imperative and specific about an essential component of evangelism. It involves the verbal proclamation of the gospel's content "to the whole creation."

THE GREAT COMMISSION IN LUKE

The next example comes from the Gospel of Luke. Luke 24:25–27, 44-49 reads:

> And he said to them, "O foolish ones, and slow of heart to believe all that the prophets have spoken! Was it not necessary that the Christ should suffer these things and enter into his glory?" And beginning with Moses and all the Prophets, He interpreted to them in all the Scriptures the things concerning himself.
>
> Then he said to them, "These are my words that I spoke to you while I was still with you, that everything written about me in the Law of Moses and the Prophets and the Psalms must be fulfilled." Then he opened their minds to understand the Scriptures, and said to them, "Thus it is written, that the Christ should suffer and on the third

day rise from the dead, and that repentance for the forgiveness of sins should be proclaimed in his name to all nations, beginning from Jerusalem. You are witnesses of these things. And behold, I am sending the promise of my Father upon you. But stay in the city until you are clothed with power from on high."

This extended passage contains two different anecdotes from the resurrection day of the Lord Jesus Christ. Two followers of Jesus were walking from Jerusalem. It was late afternoon. Jesus joined them on the walk toward the little town of Emmaus. As they were walking, they didn't recognize Him initially. They were talking about Jesus and the events of the past days, including His crucifixion.

Jesus interpreted the scriptures concerning himself, revealed His identity to them while breaking bread, and then literally vanished. Now, they became so excited that they went all the way back to Jerusalem and found the disciples gathered together. They reported what happened to them.

Just as they were talking excitedly about these things, Jesus showed up and asked them why they should be so surprised. He proceeded to give them a Bible lesson similar to the one given on the road to Emmaus. He explained how He fulfilled all the Old Testament promises regarding the Messiah, including His death and resurrection. He also pointed them to the Scriptures, which foretell that "repentance for the forgiveness of sins should be proclaimed in his name to all nations."

This encounter is a dramatic scene, but on top of that, Jesus added the Great Commission's consequential call to action. We see these elements:

- going out to all nations
- pointing to content about Christ, His death, and resurrection
- proclaiming in His name repentance for the forgiveness of sins (an essential element in Luke's record)

There is a proclamation aspect to the content of the gospel. There is also uniqueness and exclusivity in the message. The gospel of Jesus Christ is the only way to receive forgiveness of sins by repentance and faith.

THE GREAT COMMISSION IN JOHN

We see these elements again in the Gospel of John, right in the middle of Christ's high priestly prayer. John 17:18, 20–21 reads:

> "As you sent me into the world, so I have sent them into the world.
>
> I do not ask for these only, but also for those who will believe in me through their word, that they may all be one, just as you, Father, are in me, and I in you, that they also may be in us, so that the world may believe that you have sent me."

Jesus prayed, "As you sent me into the world, so I have them sent them into the world ... so that the world may believe." So, here in the Gospel of John, there is also a sending aspect. The sending is similarly purposeful with a desired result ("that the world may believe"). There's the content of "truth" in the immediate context, there's action in being sent and proclaiming "through their word," and there's direction "into the world."

Then consider the better-known statement of Christ's sending from John 20 after the resurrection. John 20:21 reads, "Jesus said to them again, 'Peace be with you. As the Father has sent me, even so I am sending you.'" This is a short but powerful statement.

THE GREAT COMMISSION IN ACTS

Now, we come to the Book of Acts, written by Luke, which also emphasizes the scene after Christ's resurrection and just before His ascension. Acts 1:6-8 reads:

> So when they had come together, they asked him, "Lord, will you at this time restore the kingdom to Israel?" He said to them, "It is not for you to know times or seasons that the Father has fixed by his own authority. But you will receive power when the Holy Spirit has come upon you, and you will be my witnesses in Jerusalem and in all Judea and Samaria, and to the end of the earth."

Consider just a few short notes on this record. Interestingly, Jesus says, in effect, "Don't worry about the end times. Worry about right now. Witnessing is My job for you: you will be My witnesses. It starts where you live now and goes through Jerusalem, Judea, Samaria, and to everywhere on earth." The Greek word meaning "witnesses" is translated in other contexts as "martyr." The context of this passage is clear that the purpose of the Holy Spirit coming is to empower Great Commission activity by witnessing to all the nations. It is also clear that Luke intended Acts to follow the formula for the geographical expansion of the church expressed in this instance of the Great Commission: Jerusalem, Judea, Samaria, and to the end of the earth.

THE GREAT COMMISSION IN MATTHEW

At last, we turn back to Matthew, which contains the best-known instance of the Great Commission. Usually, when we say "Great Commission," we mean Matthew 28:18–20:

> And Jesus came and said to them, "All authority in heaven and on earth has been given to me. Go therefore and make disciples of all nations, baptizing them in the name of the Father and of the Son and of the Holy Spirit, teaching them to observe all that I have commanded you. And behold, I am with you always, to the end of the age."

Every part of this passage is significant, but let's simply observe some of the key components.

First, Jesus states that He has been given all authority. The key verb is to "make" disciples, and the supporting verbs are "go," "baptizing," and "teaching." The reader or hearer might ask, "What does it mean to make disciples?" That question is answered and expanded on in other parts of the New Testament. A disciple is a committed follower. Making disciples begins when people hear the gospel, repent of their sins, and believe in Jesus Christ alone for their salvation. By God's grace, they have responded positively to the gospel and continue in spiritual growth as believers.

"Go" is an element in other instances of the Great Commission. What makes this one different is what happens after people have been evangelized and then become disciples.

Here in Matthew, disciples are baptized in the name of the Father, the Son, and the Holy Spirit. That's a key thought. Interestingly, there are no specific guidelines for approving a candidate for baptism besides a confirmed faith commitment to Christ for salvation. This implies that more mature believers are baptizing the new believers. New believers don't baptize themselves. Baptism is not a means of personal salvation. It is a declaration of allegiance to Christ and an entry point into a community of like-minded believers. So, we begin to see a structure within the family of believers. Church history consistently recognizes that church leaders' or, at least, mature leaders within a local congregation officiate baptisms.

The final component is "teaching them to observe all that I have commanded you." This element also has some weighty significance that we need to think about. What does "teaching them to observe all that I have commanded you" mean? And what is "all that I have commanded you"?

The reference to teaching in the mandate implies a regular meeting of saints in a local assembly of believers gathered to hear the teaching. The phrase "all that I have commanded you" does not mean only the directly quoted commands of Jesus. Instead, it means all of the things Jesus teaches and, by extension, all the teachings of the Apostles and the other authors of the New Testament—all of it is intended to be taught for the benefit of all believers. Fulfilling this part of the Great Commission requires recognizing church leaders who teach in consistent meetings of the believers.

WHAT DO YOU SEE?

So, take a step back and look at what we've considered. In the Great Commission, we have all of these elements: evangelization, discipleship, administration of church ordinances by recognized leaders, and regular meetings of believers to learn and apply the teaching of the Word of God. What we have is a local church!

The Great Commission, as found in Matthew 28, cannot be adequately fulfilled apart from planting local churches. The New Testament fills out and gives more description of the local church. A biblical local church has a mutually committed indigenous body of believers worshiping regularly around the teaching of the Word of God and prayer, observing the ordinances of baptism and communion under the leadership of biblically qualified shepherds, and actively sharing the gospel.

For the biblical local church, these elements are indigenous in the context of a particular locale and language. In other words, they are rooted in the native culture of that church's people group. Indigeneity includes the concept that the local church is self-supporting financially, self-governing by people who are leaders from among their number, and self-propagating in that they intentionally engage in gospel ministry to grow and to plant other like-minded churches in obedience to the Great Commission. The other instances of the Great Commission support this conclusion, especially in light of the greater context of the New Testament, as we will see.

A CHALLENGING APPLICATION IF WE ARE CONSISTENT

Faithfully applying this teaching comes with serious challenges. Don't let anyone tell you they are fulfilling the Great Commission simply by evangelizing and discipling. That's not the complete Great Commission. If anyone says that to you, then you should help them to understand that they are not fulfilling the Great Commission unless they are shepherding those evangelized and discipled into a Bible-teaching local church.

A second challenging aspect is the result side. You should always ask missions agencies or people involved in missions what their intended result is. Ask them about the end result even if their ministry is primarily humanitarian. We're looking for an eternal benefit for the recipients of ministry. It's OK to ask, "What are you doing with the local church? How is your ministry affecting the planting, development, establishment, or strengthening of local churches where you serve?"

Those who say they're fulfilling the Great Commission solely by doing evangelism and discipleship are falling short of complete fulfillment of the Great Commission. Ministries like that will publish statistics about how effective they are. But in our missions field experience, the statistics of those reports evaporate quickly. They are transitory and must be verified over time by an objective observer.

A dear friend and missions leader in the Philippines was bemoaning the flakey statistics published by other missions. He stated that if you believed the missions statistics published about the Philippines in our day, then every person who had ever been born in the Philippines would have been saved three times. Don't you see the foolishness of those claims? If new believers are not integrated into indigenous local churches that preach and teach God's Word with a mutually committed body of believers, then, with few exceptions, missionaries are just fooling themselves. Such fruit doesn't last.

GET TO THE POINT

Here's the point of this whole chapter: the Great Commission demonstrates the centrality of the local church as the end result in missions. We'll see much more scriptural evidence in the coming chapters.

PANICVILLE

Pastor Aaron compartmentalized his thoughts and played the part of the gracious, thankful, caring pastor as the last of his congregation left the church building. Pastors with twenty years of experience can do that. Next, he walked to his office to collect his things and thoughts as he went home for lunch. Preaching and people work can be exhilarating and exhausting at the same time. "Stunned" and "at a loss for words" were relevant descriptions of his current state of mind. Kevin and Melissa Langford had ambushed him with a sudden declaration: "We believe God is calling us into missions. We'd like Hopewell, our home church, to help us go to the field as our sending church." Pastor Aaron needed to think and pray on this after his customary Sunday afternoon nap.

He woke after a fitful rest, embarrassed about his panic. "This is a good thing, right? Shouldn't every congregation and every pastor want to have missionaries sent from their church?" he reasoned. "Surely, I learned something in seminary about this. How do we help someone become a missionary? What is our church's role in all this?" He desperately rifled through that lower shelf filled with seminary syllabi and class notes. Nothing there even mentioned those issues, much less gave guidance.

Despite the initial panic, he now knew two things. He needed to talk to his elders. And he needed to have a private conversation with the Langfords. Then there was a third and a fourth thing. He needed to pray like crazy, asking God for help. He and the church would probably need some wisdom and experience from outside the church to shine a light on this beautiful and bewildering opportunity.

THE LOCAL CHURCH IN CHRIST'S FOLLOWERS' OBEDIENCE

Inquisitive minds like to ask, "Is it so?" Inquisitive minds also want to follow this line of thought to the next logical question. Regarding what we have discussed thus far, that question is this: If the Great Commission includes local church planting as an end, did the first-century Christians hear and understand it that way? What did the original first- and secondhand hearers of the Great Commission do in obedience to this mandate?

Part of sound biblical interpretation involves trying to understand what the original author wanted to communicate to the original hearers. What was the intended response of the intended recipients? We have the record of the New Testament and a bit of history to help us.

Let's trace the obedience of the hearers through the story of the early disciples and church leaders in the Book of Acts.

THE THIRTY-THOUSAND-FOOT OVERVIEW SEES THREE MAJOR TOPICS

The Gospels close with the ascension of Christ to heaven and leave us in the hands of the inspired author, Luke, who wrote the Book of Acts as a basic history book, ending with Paul's imprisonment in Rome. We can see that the expansion of the church meant the expansion of local churches everywhere. Let's risk looking at a thirty-thousand-foot overview of the Book of Acts. We'll observe some foundational issues in the ongoing multiplication of the church. Remember that the Book of Acts is a history book. It is descriptive, not prescriptive. It is not didactic per se. It is an inspired chronology of what happened. From our vantage point, we'll identify three major topics.

THE GOSPEL

The first topic is the gospel. In the early chapters of Acts, the first Christians show us how they understood the gospel through their preaching, teaching, and interaction with the authorities and the public. Beginning with the events of the day of Pentecost, the content of the gospel is proclaimed. The focus of the gospel is Jesus Christ. The source of the gospel is the authority of Scripture and the ministry of Christ Himself. We see it in all of the interactions of the Apostles with those around them, as they refer to the Old Testament and prove that Jesus was the Messiah. They recount the miracles and the teachings of Jesus and His impact on the public in His day.

We also see the gospel's call to repentance and faith in Jesus Christ alone for salvation. It's evident that those around Jesus and those who heard the Great Commission understood that the gospel was the only means of salvation. Peter says in Acts 4:12: "There is salvation in no one else, for there is no other name under heaven given among men by which we must be saved."

THE CHURCH

The church is the second major missions issue in the Book of Acts. We see the church beginning to find its function and form, starting with Acts 2. In Acts 2:42, we read these words about the kind of fellowship people had as the church was formed: "They devoted themselves to the apostles' teaching and the fellowship, to the breaking of bread and the prayers."

The church grew at a phenomenal rate in those early weeks. We see them struggling with understanding how to care for their members. In Acts 6, we see the beginning of the idea of deacons. These "proto-deacons" were selected to help with this mercy ministry to people within the church body.

Jewish leaders envied the church. A leading Gentile figure wanted the Apostles' special authority to give the Holy Spirit. Acts 8 repeatedly uses "the church," or *ekklesia* (the called-out ones), to describe the believers in a particular location. We begin to see church diversity in chapters 8, 9, 10, and 11. These churches were multicultural rather than homogeneous. Believers from different ethnicities were gathering together as a church body. Diversity was not common in the Jewish religious culture. We see a focus on the church in Antioch and how it sends out missionaries in Acts 13. From Paul and Barnabas's first missionary journey, we see that reproducing local churches was the goal. This is especially explicit in Acts 14:21–23:

> When they had preached the gospel to that city and had made many disciples, they returned to Lystra and to

Iconium and to Antioch, strengthening the souls of the disciples, encouraging them to continue in the faith, and saying that through many tribulations we must enter the kingdom of God. And when they had appointed elders for them in every church, with prayer and fasting they committed them to the Lord in whom they had believed.

Think about it. Doesn't this perfectly mimic the pattern prescribed in the Great Commission? In every location, Paul and Barnabas evangelized, discipled, baptized, and appointed leaders to meet regularly with them for teaching from the Word of God.

Their goal was to have a mutually committed indigenous body of local believers form a church. Those groups exhibited the attributes of a local church: worshiping regularly around the teaching of the Word of God, praying together, and observing the ordinances of baptism and communion. They recognized biblically qualified leader-shepherds and actively shared the gospel in their community.

Eventually, the Council of Jerusalem affirmed that Gentiles could become believers, just like Jews, but without having to fulfill all the Jewish laws.

Fast-forward to the epistles Paul wrote to churches, and we see in those inspired letters that he thanked God that they were proclaiming the gospel, making disciples of others, and planting more churches.

MISSIONS STRATEGY

The third major area of critical missions issues is missions strategy. Acts 13 and 14 are filled with the names of towns and cities that the missionary team visited, sharing the gospel. Then they returned to establish churches and appoint leaders for them.

The missions strategy was transcultural in its message and shared fellowship. The joy of the transcultural gospel is highlighted in the reports made by Paul, Barnabas, and Peter at the Jerusalem Council, as seen in Acts 15.

They seemed to work in missionary teams rather than going alone. Qualified team members were chosen, added, or dispatched as the need arose.

Another part of Paul's strategy was contextualizing the message when needed and as appropriate. In Acts 17:2–3, we see him ministering in Thessalonica: "And Paul went in, as was his custom, and on three Sabbath days he reasoned with them from the Scriptures, explaining and proving that it was necessary for the Christ to suffer and to rise from the dead, and saying, 'This Jesus, whom I proclaim to you, is the Christ.'"

Paul went on from there to Berea and then to Athens. There, he introduced the truths of the gospel and God, starting with illustrations from Greek philosophy and references the Athenians understood.

Another element of missions strategy is the training of indigenous leaders. We see this highlighted in Acts 19 and 20, especially in Ephesus. Paul spent two years there, establishing a school of Bible theology and ecclesiology in Ephesus. Out of Ephesus, we know of other churches that Paul's students planted during that time. We understand that the training for church planters and church leaders really worked. Later, in Acts 20, Paul returns to Ephesus and instructs the elders he left there in their responsibility to shepherd, guard, and feed the flock.

The last one of these principles for missions strategy comes from an overview of Acts 21–28. It is respect for political authority.

Zipping through the Book of Acts, we can count no fewer than twenty-four churches planted from Jerusalem to Rome throughout the life and ministry of the early first-century believers. This list includes those that were planted as a result of the Apostle Paul's missionary ministry.

RECORDS FROM HISTORY

Records from church history are less reliable than the inspired Word of God, but we can still learn a great deal from church history and tradition. Here is a summary, drawn from early Christian writings and tradition, of the work of the Apostles.[4]

- During the persecution under Emperor Nero, Peter and Paul were martyred in Rome around the mid-60s AD. Paul was beheaded. Peter was crucified upside down, at his request, since he did not feel worthy to die in the same manner as the Lord Jesus Christ.

- Andrew is supposed to have gone to the area we now know as Russia. Christians there claim him as the first to bring the gospel to their location. He also preached in Asia Minor, modern-day Turkey, and Greece. He is also said to have been crucified.

- Thomas was most active in the area east of Syria. Tradition has him going as far east as India. A significant group of Christians in southern India claim Thomas as their church's founder. They claim he died there when he was pierced with spears from four soldiers.

---

4. Ken Curtis, "What Happened to the 12 Disciples and Apostles of Jesus?," Christianity.com, April 2, 2024, https://www.christianity.com/church/church-history/timeline/1-300/whatever-happened-to-the-twelve-apostles-11629558.html.

- Philip possibly had a ministry in Carthage in North Africa until God brought the wife of a Roman proconsul to salvation in Christ. The proconsul didn't like that and murdered him.

- Matthew was a tax collector and the writer of the Gospel of Matthew. He went to Persia and, some say, Ethiopia. Perhaps he followed up on that Ethiopian eunuch to whom Philip witnessed early in the Book of Acts.

- Bartholomew had widespread missionary travels across the Arabian Peninsula and East Africa, attributed to him by tradition.

- James was the son of Altius. Of the three figures named James in the New Testament, he was the least frequently mentioned. There's some confusion about which is which, but this James is reckoned to have ministered in Syria. The historian Josephus reported that he was stoned and then clubbed to death.

- Simon, the zealot, as tradition goes, ministered in Persia, where he was killed for refusing to sacrifice to the sun god.

- Matthias was the Apostle chosen to replace Judas. Tradition sends him to Syria with Andrew and then to death by burning.

- John is the only one of the Apostles generally thought by all to have died a natural death from old age. He was the church leader in the Ephesus area and is said to have cared for Mary, the mother of Jesus, as per Jesus' instruction from the cross. During Emperor Domitian's rule, John was exiled to the island of Patmos. It was there that he wrote the New Testament Book of Revelation.

IN SUMMARY

The summation of this survey is simple: both those who heard the Great Commission from Jesus and those who heard it from the original hearers all seemed to be involved in gospel ministry and the planting of indigenous churches. Someone might argue that local churches simply arise as a natural consequence of gospel witness (and thus are not a point of special emphasis in the New Testament). To counter that assumption, just ask any church planter how automatic their work feels after they are two years into the process. Local churches don't happen by evangelism alone. From everything we've studied thus far, gospel churches were always the goal of the Great Commission. The planting of local churches by the Apostles and other early Christian missionaries was intentional. Church planting was and is hard work. Churches don't arise incidentally or accidentally. To obey the Great Commission, local churches must be planted.

A BEAUTIFUL AND BEWILDERING OPPORTUNITY

Praying was easy, driven by the looming need for guidance and help. Pastor Aaron visited Kevin and Melissa Langford in their home and had a great conversation with them. They were earnest and committed to missions. They were also committed to Hopewell Bible Church. They reiterated that they would like Hopewell to be their sending church. They also were very understanding, knowing that HBC was entering uncharted territory. But Pastor Aaron wanted to do things the right way and was committed to shepherding them. He was humble enough to know that he needed to ask for help.

The following day, Pastor Aaron called a trusted friend. One of his best friends from his seminary days was also an experienced pastor. Pastor Aaron knew that his friend's church had sent some of their own members to the missions field. The friend encouraged him to get resources and help from Propempo International, which specializes in helping local churches send their missionaries well.

Pastor Aaron's friend said, "Sometimes it's constructive to get some trusted wisdom and expertise from outside your own church's normal circle of relationships. You don't see what you're not seeing. You don't know what you don't know. This is especially true when your church needs to change or adjust much faster than normal to meet a particular issue or opportunity. A coach and teacher who resonates with our doctrine and has a local-church-oriented philosophy can accelerate the process and solutions much faster than you can on your own. It's worth investing time and resources to initiate a relationship with expert help. You'll save time, effort, and the cost of mistakes. It was worth it for me and my church! Look at it this way: it's not a problem; it's an opportunity to grow in grace."

After the call, Pastor Aaron thought about how he would bring the elders up to speed at their next regular meeting.

THE LOCAL CHURCH IN CHRIST'S "ALL" OF THE NEW TESTAMENT

Before His ascension, our Lord Jesus Christ repeatedly instructed His followers to proclaim His gospel message to all nations. They and, by extension, all believers, were to witness to the entire world about His life, death, and resurrection. Jesus Himself was clear that the Old Testament foretold details of salvation in Him.

In Matthew 28:20, as we have seen, Jesus spoke of "teaching them to observe all that I have commanded you." The question is this: What is meant by "all that I have commanded you"? It's an honest question. Initially, someone might think that Jesus referred only to the words He spoke directly to His followers. But we don't have a record of everything He said publicly and privately. What we do have is the God-inspired record of the New Testament.

Another misconception is that the "all" is limited to only those things Christ communicated privately to the eleven disciples. This supposition dissolves with a closer examination of clear texts. One hermeneutical principle teaches us to use clear texts to interpret less clear ones.

We know from Christ's words in John 14, 16, and 17 that the "all" referred to in the Great Commission is what we now hold in our hands as the New Testament. Follow this flow of thought from these passages:

> 14:15: "If you love me, you will keep my commandments."

> 14:25-26: "These things I have spoken to you while I am still with you. But the Helper, the Holy Spirit, whom the Father will send in my name, he will teach you all things and bring to your remembrance all that I have said to you."

> 16:12–15: "I still have many things to say to you, but you cannot bear them now. When the Spirit of truth comes, he will guide you into all the truth, for he will not speak on his own authority, but whatever he hears he will speak, and he will declare to you the things that are to come. He will glorify me, for he will take what is mine and declare it to you. All that the Father has is mine; therefore I said that he will take what is mine and declare it to you."

> 17:8 [praying to the Father]: "For I have given them the words that you gave me, and they have received them."

> 17:17-21 [praying to the Father]: "Sanctify them in the truth; your word is truth. As you sent me into the world, so I have sent them into the world. And for their sake I consecrate myself, that they also may be sanctified in truth. I do not ask for these only, but also for those who will believe in me through their word, that they may all be one, just as you, Father, are in me, and I in you, that

they also may be in us, so that the world may believe that you have sent me."

Contributing to our understanding are the standard key New Testament passages on the inspiration of the Scriptures (e.g., 1 Corinthians 2:13; 2 Timothy 3:16–17; Hebrews 1:1–2; 1 Peter 1:10–11; 2 Peter 1:19–21; 3:15–16; 1 John 1:3, 5).

Then add the fact that Paul received direct revelation or inspiration from Christ about principles for marriage (1 Corinthians 7), instruction regarding the Lord's Supper (1 Corinthians 11), exercise of spiritual gifts (1 Corinthians 14), and giving and receiving (Acts 20:35). There are many other such claims by the human authors of the New Testament speaking as from Christ under the inspiration of the Holy Spirit.

So, all the inspired Scriptures are the "commands" of God. The New Testament is in a special sense the "commands" of Christ. Through the inspiration of the Holy Spirit, the whole New Testament becomes the "all that I have commanded you" referred to in the Great Commission.

WHY IS THIS "ALL" SO IMPORTANT TO THE LOCAL CHURCH'S ROLE IN MISSIONS?

We're taking time to examine this aspect of the Great Commission closely because:

1. We tend to skim over it too quickly to really understand it.

2. Subsequently, we fail to understand the Great Commission in the same way the original hearers understood it.

3. As a result, we become unable to see the connection to the local church.

The original hearers of the Great Commission (and its variants) understood that obedience to it resulted in the creation of local churches everywhere. The Great Commission didn't end with the evangelism of new believers. It wasn't even completed through the discipleship of believers. The end result was a body of believers observing the ordinances, having leaders, and worshiping together regularly under the teaching of God's Word.

When we understand this simple truth correctly, it focuses our attention on the local church as the desired goal of missions. Missions begins and ends with local churches.

ARE WE STRETCHING THE POINT?

In emphasizing the local church to this degree, we are simply highlighting what we see in the Bible. The canon of the New Testament itself shows us what is hidden in plain sight: all the epistles were written to local churches or leaders of local churches and were intended to be obeyed by their readers in the context of local churches.

If we take a step back and look at the entire New Testament—the authors and the recipients alike—we see the work of the Holy Spirit in inspiring the tapestry that is woven together to reinforce this principle. Not only is the local church central in missions, but the local church is central in God's whole plan.

Think about it. The Holy Spirit inspired Matthew to write the Gospel of Matthew. Tradition says that Matthew went to Persia and Ethiopia. Thus, in addition to writing the best-known version of the Great Commission, he obeyed it by going and bringing the gospel of Jesus Christ to other lands. We know that churches were planted there, probably by Matthew and others.

Mark, another Gospel author, is a fascinating character. He was not an Apostle, but he had a close association with Peter. In fact, Peter mentions Mark in 1 Peter 5:13 as being his protégé or helper. We also know that Mark went on the first missionary journey of Saul (who became more widely known as Paul) and Barnabas. Mark deserted that journey, leading Paul and Barnabas to argue about whether he should accompany them on a second missionary journey. Mark then joined up with Barnabas, whose name means "the son of encouragement." Paul chose Silas, and the split team went their separate ways. Much later, Paul remarks that Mark was useful to him and desired to have Mark visit him in Rome. Again, from tradition, Mark accompanied Peter to Rome and spent much time with him before Peter was martyred there. That was around the same time that Paul was also in Rome. The point is this: Mark was involved in church planting ministry due to his relationship with Barnabas and his obedience to Christ.

Luke, the author of another Gospel and the Book of Acts, is a very interesting character as well. We know little about Luke except that he seemed to have had medical training of some kind. He is often referred to as Dr. Luke in Bible commentaries. Luke was a protégé of Paul. He came into Paul's circle around the time of the second missionary journey during the visit to Troas. We see him in the missionary team just before they went to Europe and began ministry in Philippi. Luke is the chronicler of the Book of Acts, the church history book of the first century. You can tell when he is in the traveling group by his use of the personal pronouns "us" or "we," in contrast to "they" or "them." Luke had the inside scoop on all of Paul's work, ministry, and relationships. He faithfully recorded this in the Book of Acts for our understanding and edification. Luke was integral to Paul's missionary team in church planting and leadership development.

We know quite a bit about John and John's Gospel. We also know that he wrote later epistles and the Book of Revelation. He had a longstanding ministry of proclaiming the gospel of Jesus Christ and seeing churches established. While living on the northern edge of Ephesus, John would have had a personal connection with each of the seven churches mentioned in the early chapters of Revelation. We see from church history and his writings, particularly the epistles and the first part of the Book of Revelation, how dear local churches were to John's heart.

The Book of Acts, as we have seen, shows how local churches were developed and planted in cities around the eastern half of the Mediterranean. Bible teachers agree that Luke's record of the Great Commission in Acts 1:8 outlines the Book of Acts. The church and the gospel went forth from Jerusalem to Judea, Samaria, and (in a process that is still ongoing) the ends of the earth.

Now, we get into the letters of the New Testament. Most were written by the Apostle Paul, a missionary church planter. Every book Paul wrote in the inspired Scripture is addressed to churches or church leaders. This is also true of the recipients of all the epistles in a more general sense. But let's look at the epistles one at a time.

Romans was written to churches planted in Rome, perhaps reinforced by Peter's ministry there. Paul wanted the Roman church to understand the gospel with great clarity and know its place in history. He also wrote about the inner workings and dynamics of the church. We see, for example, in Romans 12, so many "one another" commands. These are just a few of the many "one another" commands throughout the epistles of Paul and other letters in the New Testament.

Recall that a Christian cannot obey the "one another" commands without being part of a mutually committed body of Christ. No one can do all the "one anothers" with the universal church at large.

We know from the closing chapters of Acts that as Paul went to Rome, he connected with several churches that helped him on his way from the port to the capital city of Rome. In Romans 16:16, he uses this phrase: "All the churches of Christ greet you." There are three specific churches mentioned and something like thirty people that Paul named before he ever went to Rome. Then, at the very end of the letter, he names eight fellow workers. So Romans 16 is full of names and full of churches.

Let's pick up the pace and make observations about other epistles. In 1 and 2 Corinthians, Paul addresses the severe problems of the church in Corinth. Yet he had great affection for the church and its leaders. He encourages them to hold fast to the teaching that he gave them about how the church should operate regarding order in its worship, communion, and so forth. So he's addressing specific church-life issues.

Galatians was written to a group of churches in the area of Galatia that, we believe, were struggling with understanding the gospel clearly. They needed Paul's help to understand the priority of the gospel, especially the imperative not to add something to it.

Then we come to Ephesians. This letter is majestic in so many ways. It mentions the church a lot. We'll refer to more from Ephesians 3 later.

Philippians is the only letter that mentions both elders and deacons in the early greeting. Clearly, this church was dear to Paul and had a longstanding part in his financial support.

Colossians is the twin epistle of Ephesians. It is also very rich in describing the church and the effectiveness of its ministry in taking the gospel to other places.

Two very early letters in Paul's writings, 1 and 2 Thessalonians, are clear with regard to matters in that church's life.

Finally, we come to Paul's pastoral epistles: 1 and 2 Timothy and Titus. These are specific instructions to protégés of Paul who had been in long-term ministry with him and received training, discipleship, and mentoring to do church work. Timothy was the younger pastor of the church of Ephesus, a very influential church. And Titus was asked to do the hard work of setting the churches in order on the island of Crete.

Philemon was also a church leader. Paul wrote him about a personal request. A lot of warmth is communicated in the letter. The matter of Paul's concern is connected with the church and Christian brotherhood.

Now, the general epistles: Hebrews; James; 1 and 2 Peter; 1, 2, and 3 John; and Jude. Hebrews and James specifically mention church issues and church leaders. They were written primarily to Jewish believers who were scattered. Still, they focus on the church and church issues. They address things like attending worship services together, not neglecting to fellowship together during those services, honoring and respecting elders in the church, and not showing favoritism or bias toward different kinds of people coming into the church worship service. They also instruct those who are sick to call for the elders to pray for them.

Peter gives specific instructions and qualifications for church leadership in his letters. John talks more generally about the characteristics of a genuine believer. We would extend that to mean one who qualifies as a genuine convert and is allowed to fellowship as a church member. In 3 John, he's explicitly addressing a church leader concerning a couple of issues, one of which is the key issue of support and sending out missionaries.

Jude addresses church leaders to deal with people who have crept in with false teaching. The process, which involves both leadership and membership, consists of taking steps toward correction and not allowing false teaching to cause division in the church.

Of course, we've already glanced at the Book of Revelation and those first three chapters that mention particular things about local churches and Christ's love for and protection of them. They are so dear to our Lord Jesus Christ that He gives specific instructions about correcting how they function as a church.

You've probably heard the truism many times before that it's hard to see the forest for the trees. In other words, sometimes we get so focused on just what's in front of us that we don't see the big picture. Right now, we advocate for the forest view. Take a look at the New Testament. Church planters wrote all of the New Testament to local churches and believers scattered everywhere. They loved the local church.

They saw God's amazing new creation in Christ through the gospel: assemblies of believers in local places everywhere they went. These local churches demonstrated Christ, proclaimed Christ, showed Christ in their interactions, and grew together in Christ as a body.

The New Testament is about the local church, and the local church should be the focus of missions from beginning to end. Those of us in missions should love the local church because Christ loved the local church. The Apostles loved the local church. The writers of the New Testament loved the local church. The canon of the New Testament itself displays this truth. All of the known authors of the New Testament's books were church planters. All the epistles were written to local churches or leaders of local churches and were intended to be obeyed by their readers in the context of local churches. Once you see this big picture, it's hard to unsee it.

When Christ speaks of "all that I have commanded you" in the Great Commission, His "all" includes the whole of the New Testament. The books of the New Testament were written for and about the local church. Therefore, the local church lies at the center of "all" that Christians are called to teach.

GETTING UP TO SPEED

Pastor Aaron's meeting with the elders went better than he had expected. He brought them up to speed on Kevin and Melissa Langford's desire to be missionaries. The elders were very excited about that. But the discussion split over the all-important details of the Langfords' request.

"We'd like Hopewell to be our sending church," they had said, "to enable us to go to the missions field." The elders asked themselves, "How are we to be involved in preparing them for the field? Isn't that the missions agency's responsibility? Which field in particular? How much is it going to cost us? Is Hopewell expected to provide all their support? What does it mean to 'send' a missionary?" So many questions, so little experience and understanding.

The elders wholeheartedly charged Pastor Aaron to call the specialists that his pastor friend had recommended. Pastor Aaron made the call to Propempo International. The conversation lasted forty minutes, with a lot of questions on both sides. Contact information, some immediate tasks, and a promise of email communication were exchanged.

Aaron left the call impressed, relieved, and hopeful. "The organization certainly has a solid background of working with churches and missionaries," Aaron thought. They have been helping churches in missions for decades. In addition to being committed to biblical principles, they also had respect for the unique history and immediate concerns of Hopewell Bible Church. They wanted to tap extensive knowledge about missions from the local church perspective to serve HBC's needs best. They have come alongside many churches to help them do this very thing: send their members as missionaries to strategic missions ministries worldwide.

Pastor Aaron was surprised that HBC was expected to do some homework. HBC was not entering a one-size-fits-all, formulaic program. Propempo International wanted to know specifics about Hopewell's connections and commitments in missions, asking questions like:

- What structures does HBC have for missions? A missions leader? A Missions Team (or Committee)?

- How much of HBC's giving income is designated for missions?

- Who and what is supported by HBC missions funds? How much does each entity receive per year? What is their/its relationship to the church? Where are those ministries located?

- What is HBC's doctrine, vision, and values? How does that impact (or not impact) the missions ministries Hopewell presently supports?

- Does HBC know where the Langfords want to serve in

missions and their long-term goals? Does HBC even care about those details? Why or why not?

- Does HBC have a special relationship with a particular missions agency or missionary ministry it already knows and loves?

These questions prepared everyone for the mutually agreed upon intensive training and planning weekend with Propempo's missions coaching staff. The goal of the session, which would last from Friday evening into Sunday, was to help HBC move forward. All the elders, the Langfords, and Missions Team members would participate.

Aaron felt like he was back in serious student mode again. This whole scenario would entail an intense learning curve for him, the elders, the Langfords, and everyone involved.

THE LOCAL CHURCH IN THE APOSTLE PAUL'S VIEW

Even before Saul of Tarsus became a follower and ardent disciple of Jesus Christ, he was aware that local bodies of believers were vital to the growth of the Way. Each church was a locus of devotion to Christ and a witness to Jesus' gospel, propagating Christ's teaching, along with mutual fellowship and encouragement, in the face of Saul's persecution. It says in Acts 8:3 that "Saul was ravaging the church."

After his conversion in Acts 9, he became aware of churches in Jerusalem, Judea, and Samaria. From the beginning of Paul's life as a Christian, we see that he respectfully deferred to local church leadership in Damascus. God instructed him, and the church helped him escape threats to his life in Damascus. After three years in the wilderness of Arabia, he returned to Damascus and fellowshipped with the church again.

PAUL WAS TUTORED BY JESUS CHRIST

One of the critical questions you must ask is what happened to Paul between the time he fled from Damascus and his return to Damascus approximately three years later. The short answer to that question is that Paul became an Apostle. What does that mean? It means that he had personal contact with Jesus Christ Himself. A passage in Galatians 1, data from the Book of Acts, Paul's statements in Ephesians 3, and several comments to churches in his letters about explicit instruction from Christ show that he had direct contact with Jesus. Paul maintains that, although he was the last of the Apostles (and called himself the least of them), he was nevertheless a full Apostle (Galatians 1:11–17; 2:1–9).

When he went to Jerusalem to spend time with Peter and James (Galatians 2:7–9), Paul came as a peer, a colleague, and a fellow Apostle. That office and status was never questioned by the original twelve. His status as an Apostle was key to his ministry. It also becomes a key to our understanding of Paul's view of the local church.

Let's review what Paul says about himself being an Apostle:

- Romans 1:1: "Paul, a servant of Christ Jesus, called to be an apostle, set apart for the gospel of God…"
- Romans 11:13: "Now I am speaking to you Gentiles. In as much as I am an apostle to the Gentiles…"
- 1 Corinthians 1:1: "Paul, called by the will of God to be an apostle of Christ Jesus…"
- 1 Corinthians 9:1: "Am I not free? Am I not an apostle? Have I not seen Jesus our Lord?"
- 1 Corinthians 9:2: "If to others I am not an apostle, at least I am to you, for you are the seal of my apostleship in the Lord."
- 1 Corinthians 15:9: "For I am the least of the apostles, unworthy to be called an apostle, because I persecuted the church of God."

- 2 Corinthians 1:1: "Paul, an apostle of Christ Jesus by the will of God…to the church of God that is at Corinth…"
- 2 Corinthians 12:12: "The signs of a true apostle were performed among you with utmost patience."
- Galatians 1:1: "Paul, an apostle—not from men, nor through man, but through Jesus Christ and God the Father, who raised Him from the dead…"
- Ephesians 1:1: "Paul, an apostle of Christ Jesus by the will of God…"
- Colossians 1:1: "Paul, an apostle of Christ Jesus by the will of God…"
- 1 Timothy 1:1: "Paul, an apostle of Christ Jesus by command of God our Savior and of Christ Jesus our hope…"
- 1 Timothy 2:7: "For this I was appointed a preacher and an apostle…a teacher of the Gentiles in faith and truth…"
- 2 Timothy 1:1, 11: "Paul, an apostle of Christ Jesus by the will of God…for which I was appointed a preacher and an apostle and teacher…"
- Titus 1:1: "Paul, a servant of God and an apostle of Jesus Christ, for the sake of the faith of God's elect and their knowledge of the truth…"

Paul was an Apostle because he was called, appointed, and sent out by Jesus Christ personally as one of His Apostles. He spent time with Jesus Christ. Paul lived in Jerusalem contemporaneously with the ministry of Jesus Christ, and he knew of Jesus' ministry even to other parts of Israel.

PAUL'S CALLING TO LOCAL CHURCH MINISTRY

Paul, referring to his calling in Ephesians 3–4 and Galatians 1, understood that he was given specific privilege and responsibility to organize churches according to Christ's private and personal teaching. Paul's conversion came through a post-resurrection appearance of Jesus Christ to him on the road to Damascus and a later encounter with Jesus in the wilderness during those three years.

Years later, Barnabas recruited Paul to help establish the church in Antioch. Note that Paul knew he was called to be a missionary but waited almost twelve years after his conversion for the church leaders of Antioch to agree to send him and Barnabas out as missionaries from the church. He submitted to the Antioch church elders to send him as a missionary.

Throughout his ministry, Paul prioritized church planting, training church leaders, and mentoring in all aspects of church life, worship, order, and liturgy. In heaven, we might find it fascinating to ask Paul to show us his "Minister's Manual," the training manual for how ministers were to conduct the services and order of the church.

PAUL'S BOOK OF ORDER FOR LOCAL CHURCHES

Here's what Paul did through his writings. He set in order:

- church corporate worship meetings
- the content of church worship meetings
- qualifications and selection or appointment of church leaders, specifically elders and deacons
- church members' roles

- church organizational structure
- prayer in corporate meetings
- the roles of men and women in the church and life
- the authority of the church
- the primacy of Bible reading, teaching, and exhortation in the church
- details about church ordinances, the Lord's Supper, and baptism
- spiritual growth and mutual accountability in the church
- the importance of unity, fellowship, and forgiveness in the local church
- spiritual discipline, exercised in and by the local church
- the dynamics of church members' interactions as a body
- the centrality of the church to Christian life, worship, and maturity
- the headship of Christ over the church and its leaders
- the role and tasks of the church leaders in feeding, guarding, and leading the flock
- financial support for vocational church leaders
- giving in and through the local church to both internal and external causes
- missions through the church
- the sending role of the local church for missions
- the leader's role in equipping the saints for the ministries of the church

- Sunday as the normal day for corporate worship and the gathering of the saints
- use of music in corporate worship

By extension, Paul set forth the centrality of the local church as God's means for Christian teaching, gospel transformation, witness, worship, fellowship, mutual growth, and accountability.

PAUL'S PASSION FOR PIONEER CHURCH PLANTING

Paul made multiple references to the church's role in sending out gospel workers, including himself. He asked the church in Rome to send him to the unreached area of Spain and used the word *propempo*. It means to send forward or to send out.

Toward the end of Paul's life, while he was in prison in Rome, he reflected on his ministry when writing his letter to the Ephesians. In Ephesians 3:8-10, he tells us he was charged to do two things:

> To me, though I am the very least of all the saints, this grace was given, to preach to the Gentiles the unsearchable riches of Christ, and to bring to light for everyone what is the plan of the mystery hidden for ages in God, who created all things, so that through the church the manifold wisdom of God might now be made known to the rulers and authorities in the heavenly places.

These two things—preaching and teaching—were his calling. He was consistent throughout his whole life's ministry in preaching "the unsearchable riches of Christ" and teaching the administration of the local church. As we read this passage, we tend to focus on his ministry of preaching "to the Gentiles" and miss his administrative pastoral ministry of planting and organizing local churches according to God's instruction.

How do we know that Paul was also focused on the local church? It's obvious, if we avoid missing the forest for the trees. Look at his letters: Romans, 1 and 2 Corinthians, Galatians, Ephesians, Philippians, Colossians, 1 and 2 Thessalonians, 1 and 2 Timothy, Titus, and Philemon.

All the letters he wrote were to local churches and local church leaders. And Paul filled those letters with specific information about church issues. Paul kept reminding them, "I told you about this; I told you about that," concerning the worship manual of the church. Paul's library of letters to churches closes with the pastoral letters, which contain his final words of encouragement, strategy, and training for the local church and pastoral ministry, both in a well-established urban church setting with Timothy at Ephesus and in a more pioneering setting in Crete and eventually (for Titus) Dalmatia. He also issued a call to action before he arrived in Rome for the Roman church to send him forward (*propempo*) to the unreached area of Spain.

So, in Paul's view, it was clear God intended for the expansion and expression of the gospel to be through the church and, we can say, through local churches. That, not the anonymous universal church, was where the action was—and is! It is through local churches that, as Paul wrote in Ephesians 3:10–11, "the manifold wisdom of God might now be made known to the rulers and authorities in the heavenly places. This was according to the eternal purpose that he has realized in Christ Jesus our Lord."

Paul understood that his commission was to preach the gospel, to plant and strengthen churches that preach the gospel and plant other churches. How do we know that?

Look at Ephesians 3:20–21: "Now to him who is able to do far more abundantly than all that we ask or think, according to the power at work within us, to him be glory in the church and in Christ Jesus throughout all generations, forever and ever. Amen." If our hermeneutic is correct, we can paraphrase the end of the passage as, "Be glory in local churches everywhere in Christ Jesus, throughout all generations, forever and ever. Amen."

Paul saw that the local church was always God's plan for magnifying His wisdom and the glory of Jesus Christ forever and ever. The local church was the means of missions, and it was the result of missions for Paul.

PAUL WAITING FOR ANTIOCH TO SEND HIM OUT

It's amusing to consider what the Apostle Paul might think about some generally accepted assumptions in today's missions world. Take the issues of calling, for example. For Paul, a missionary wasn't somebody who said that they had some special call to do any undefined something in a cross-cultural context. For Paul, a missionary was recognized and commended by local church leaders. Paul would say, "Don't go unless you are sent!"

Just like he waited for at least twelve years to get that commendation from his elders at Antioch, Paul would expect today's missionary candidates to earn recognition within their own local church as sufficiently experienced, godly, mature Christians going out with the purpose of planting indigenous local churches capable of reproducing local churches. Understanding Paul this way changes how we implement missions for local churches across the board. It changes the roles of the church missions leader, the candidates and missionaries, the missions agencies, the missions donors, and the missionary-training institutions.

There is another example in the disparity of the way people think about the goal of missions. Everyone wants to claim that their missions methodology follows Pauline practice. Yet few embrace and implement two key threads from our study here:

1. Paul was a local church planter. Though he was a missionary by calling, his methodology to change the world was simply to plant local churches. Paul's heart priority was a healthy local church.

2. Paul's missions goal and methodology was to establish local churches. His missiology was his ecclesiology. If Paul had not had this focus according to God's plan, would the gospel have reached our part of the world yet?

If we understand Paul correctly, it seems that:

- You can't have a biblical missiology without a healthy ecclesiology.

- And you can't have a biblical ecclesiology without a healthy missiology.

We all must recalibrate the prescription of our ministry lenses to focus on the biblical centrality of the local church in missions. It will change the way we do missions for the better.

THE INTENSE LEARNING CURVE

Much to the surprise and relief of Pastor Aaron and the elders, the training and planning weekend with Propempo International went really well. With some guidance, the Hopewell Bible Church leaders clarified their biblical values and definitions of missions. They got a biblically informed view of their church's role in missions. In their own words, they reaffirmed the theological and biblical basis for how HBC would do missions moving forward. In the New Testament, they saw teaching and models for the local church's importance in missions.

In the process, it became evident how Hopewell needed to come alongside the Langfords to send them to the missions field. The weekend was an intense, focused learning time of putting the pieces together to see the outlines of the bigger puzzle. Now that they had established the puzzle framework and an idea of the major parts, they could find and fit the remaining pieces together to finish the puzzle.

Praise God, the elders of HBC were unified in moving forward! The intensive weekend process laid the foundation for development. But there was still a lot of work to do.

- The Missions Team needed information and education about the coming changes.

- The presently supported missionaries and ministries also needed to be informed about HBC renewing and refocusing its missions vision. Those not aligning with HBC's doctrine and priorities might need to be graciously released from continuing financial partnership. Those with a history of relationship with the church who are not yet aligned with this new direction might need to be grandfathered for a while.

- The Langfords needed significant training and preparation in many ways: character, calling, conviction, and competencies. (See appendix B on missionary training). Even if they could be dedicated full-time to training, it might still take two to three years. If only part-time, it could significantly take longer.

- The congregation needed teaching from the leaders about HBC's understanding of missions from the Bible, including the priority of the local church in missions.

- The congregation needed a biblically informed orientation to their role as a sending church that would come alongside the Langfords in prayer, encouragement, counsel, and many other practical ways.

- Specific action steps were needed to plan and resource the Langfords' training and development as missionaries before they were confirmed and commissioned to go to the field.

The elders were exhilarated. Pastor Aaron was encouraged. The Langfords were exhausted! Kevin and Melissa realized what they started had exploded into something more significant than they had expected. But it was also more glorious. Yes, it was going to take a lot of work. But the result, Lord willing, would be so much better than what they had originally hoped for.

The HBC leaders, the church family, and the Langfords could now confidently face the future together.

THE LOCAL CHURCH IN GOD THE FATHER'S VIEW

Now, let's look at the role of the local church from God's perspective. First, we should consider the Trinity. The Trinity is God the Father, God the Son, and God the Holy Spirit. All three persons of the Trinity were and are involved in every aspect of creation, redemption, the inspiration of the Scriptures, the fulfillment of all the prophecies and promises of inspired Scripture, the final judgment, and the ultimate comprehensive worship of the Lord Jesus Christ for eternity.

We understand that all three persons of the Trinity are involved in God's timeless plan for His glory. Father, Son, and Holy Spirit are behind the inspiration of the Bible that is in our hands. Everything written there has been spoken, secured, and safeguarded by all three persons of the Trinity. God speaks, Christ speaks, and the Holy Spirit speaks to us through the Bible.

All that the Bible teaches, God teaches. It is eternal; it is true; it will accomplish His purposes, as Isaiah 55:11 says. The Bible is self-authenticating and testifies that it expresses God's will and ways forever.

Psalm 119:89 states, "Forever, O LORD, your word is firmly fixed in the heavens." Psalm 119:152 reads, "Long have I known from your testimonies that you have founded them forever." Psalm 119:160 says, "The sum of your word is truth, and every one of your righteous rules endures forever." In Matthew 24:35, Jesus declares, "Heaven and earth will pass away, but my words will not pass away."

We are reminded that everything we have studied from the Bible thus far has been God's view of the local church's role in missions. We can find seeds of local church ecclesiology and the scope of missiology in many Old Testament references to the called-out assembly of God's people. God makes provision for people from every tongue, tribe, and nation in the brotherhood of priests, including non-Hebrews worshiping God; this is an extension of His mercy and grace to the nations. One thousand times, apart from specific condemnation and judgment passages, terms like "the nations," "all peoples," and "all the earth" are mentioned in the context of including them in God's blessings. Psalm 67 is just one outstanding example of this. It reads:

> May God be gracious to us and bless us
> and make his face to shine upon us,
>
> that your way may be known *on earth*,
> your saving power *among all nations*.
>
> Let *the peoples* praise you, O God;
> let *all the peoples* praise you!
>
> Let *the nations* be glad and sing for joy,
> for you judge *the peoples* with equity
> and guide the nations upon earth.

> Let *the peoples* praise you, O God;
> let *all the peoples* praise you!
>
> The earth has yielded its increase;
> God, our God, shall bless us.
>
> God shall bless us;
> let *all the ends of the earth* fear him!

WHAT JESUS SAYS GOD SAYS

Then, as the new covenant dawns with the incarnation of the Lord Jesus Christ, we receive more precise directions about the local church. When Jesus says in Matthew 16:18, "I will build my church," *God* says it. God gives instructions through Jesus' teaching to the church in Matthew 18 related to purity, membership, and authority in the local church.

God creates the church and appoints Christ as head per Ephesians 1:22–23: "And he put all things under his feet and gave him as head over all things to the church, which is his body, the fullness of him who fills all in all."

God is the designer of the church and of Christ's headship of the church per Colossians 1:18: "And he is head of the body, the church."

PAUL REFERS TO GOD THE FATHER'S VIEW

Under divine inspiration, Paul frequently referenced the church of God in the salutation of his letters:

- Romans 1:7: "To all those in Rome who are loved by God and called to be saints: Grace to you and peace from God our Father."

- 1 Corinthians 1:2: "To the church of God that is in Corinth…" (It is not inconsequential that he references the church of God and leads with God the Father in his greetings to the churches.)
- 2 Corinthians 1:1: "To the church of God that is at Corinth…"
- Galatians 1:2-3: "To the churches of Galatia: Grace to you and peace from God our Father."
- Ephesians 1:2: "Grace to you and peace from God our Father." (Paul uses the same phrase in Philippians 1:2 and in Colossians 1:2.)
- 1 Thessalonians 1:1: "To the church of the Thessalonians in God the Father…"
- 2 Thessalonians 1:1: "To the church of the Thessalonians in God our Father…"
- Verse 1:2 of both 1 and 2 Timothy: "Grace, mercy, and peace from God the Father."
- Titus 1:4: "Grace and peace from God the Father."
- Philemon 1:3: "Grace to you and peace from God our Father."

The Apostle Paul, like the other human authors of the New Testament, includes God the Father in every aspect of Christian salvation, life, worship, and assembly. The local church was and is His plan. The Scriptures repeatedly include God the Father as the church's founder-participant, if you will, placing Christ at its head. All these passages are clear through explicit and implicit reference to God's part in the church and God's care for the church.

THE BIG PLAN OF GOD THE FATHER REVEALED

The clincher passage, in our view, is Ephesians 3. Paul is writing his testimony and reflecting at the end of his life about his calling and his work. Let's take a closer look at this key passage. The central concept is that God gets the glory in the church. He designed the local church to show His wisdom and to result in His glory.

Ephesians 3:7–11, 20–21 reads:

> Of this gospel I was made a minister according to the gift of God's grace, which was given me by the working of his power. To me, though I am the very least of all the saints, this grace was given, to preach to the Gentiles the unsearchable riches of Christ, and to bring to light for everyone what is the plan of the mystery hidden for ages in God, who created all things, so that through the church the manifold wisdom of God might now be made known to the rulers and authorities in the heavenly places. This was according to the eternal purpose that he has realized in Christ Jesus our Lord....
>
> Now to him who is able to do far more abundantly than all that we ask or think, according to the power at work within us, to him be glory in the church and in Christ Jesus throughout all generations, forever and ever. Amen.

There are five ways that God's glory in the church surprises us and exceeds our expectations in this passage:

1. The church is the central agent in God's plan (vv. 9–11).

2. The church is a primary means of displaying God's wisdom (v.10).

3. The church has been God's plan A forever; no plan B exists (v. 11).

4. God's plans for the church far exceed our expectations of results (vv. 20–21).

5. God's glory in the church far exceeds our expectations of time (v. 21).

We've seen previously that, when reading Paul, the default sense of "church" should typically cause us to think of "local church." Conversely, the default understanding of the word "church" should not be understood to mean "universal or invisible church" except where the context demands it. *Local* church(es) should be the default way to read the use of "church" in the rest of the New Testament as well. Failure to do so diminishes our understanding of, and appreciation for, God's purposes for the local church, as humble and flawed as each local church may be.

Likewise, we see part of God's design expanded later in Ephesians 5. Note that this particular context does demand that "the church" and "her/she" be read as the universal church. Still, the visible expression of the above comes through the local church. Ephesians 5:25–32 states:

> Husbands, love your wives, as Christ loved the church and gave himself up for her, that he might sanctify her, having cleansed her by the washing of water with the word, so that he might present the church to himself in splendor, without spot or wrinkle or any such thing,

that she might be holy and without blemish. In the same way husbands should love their wives as their own bodies. He who loves his wife loves himself. For no one ever hated his own flesh, but nourishes and cherishes it, just as Christ does the church, because we are members of his body. "Therefore a man shall leave his father and mother and hold fast to his wife, and the two shall become one flesh." This mystery is profound, and I am saying that it refers to Christ and the church.

We see another glimpse of God's activity and purpose in the church in Colossians 1:24–28:

> Now I rejoice in my sufferings for your sake, and in my flesh I am filling up what is lacking in Christ's afflictions for the sake of his body, that is, the church, of which I became a minister according to the stewardship from God that was given to me for you, to make the word of God fully known, the mystery hidden for ages and generations but now revealed to his saints. To them God chose to make known how great among the Gentiles are the riches of the glory of this mystery, which is Christ in you, the hope of glory. Him we proclaim, warning everyone and teaching everyone with all wisdom, that we may present everyone mature in Christ.

THE FATHER'S MISSIONS INTENTIONS IN THE LOCAL CHURCH

There is a missions context and intention in these passages. Mutual discipleship and spiritual growth are not the only aims in view. God also intends that onlookers, visitors, and the general public see the supernatural affection, unity, and instruction in God's Word, as well as the "one anothers" in action, producing gracious, loving, Christ-honoring people because of their membership in their local church.

God has purposed that the local church is His means, His agent on earth, for fulfilling His mission. That's the local church's mission. It's not just the centrality of the local church in missions; it's the centrality of the local church in all God's purposes on earth. Is it too much to say that, while missio Dei (the "mission of God") is bigger than local churches everywhere, local churches are at the center of His "missio"?

FACING THE FUTURE

Having a destination goal and a road map is one thing. Making the journey is another. The elders and congregation were excited about the future with the Langfords. But stepping up with the Langfords was a big commitment. Still, having biblical clarity about Hopewell's role in doing this was refreshing. It brought along confidence and a sense of heading in the right direction.

Just like with a long-anticipated family road trip, there was a lot of planning, preparation, and packing to do. Sending someone as a missionary to an unreached people group (UPG) is not something left to chance. The well-being of your sent missionary family is a significant shepherding concern for real people. The spiritual well-being of the target ministry group has eternal consequences. "As the Spirit leads" is not a plan. The Spirit can and will lead the leaders as they make a plan. "Failing to plan is planning to fail," as the saying goes.

Some of the nitty-gritty elements of sending came into play for the congregation, as they applied in practical ways what had been learned from the church engagement coach and the recommended resources. So, the elders created a general list of significant steps forward into the future:

1. Pastor Aaron would start a new six-week preaching series on the local church's role in missions to give the congregation a biblical vision and express his support for and solidarity with future changes.

2. Hopewell's refreshed missions direction and focus, including the sending of the Langfords, would regularly be on the church prayer list.

3. Pastor Aaron would communicate with all the presently supported missionaries and ministries, asking for their prayer and cooperation as the church strode toward and implemented fresh ideals.

4. The Missions Team would begin to read, study, and listen as they discerned how sending the Langfords would impact and change their guiding principles and policies.

5. The elders would work with the Missions Team to identify the congregation's relationships, skills, and interests in the process of identifying a strategic missions focus for the church.

6. The Langfords and the Missions Team would be charged with developing a timeline for their missionary preparation. Milestones would include identifying a specific field, partner missions agency, and ministry for their future work.

With so many new things happening simultaneously, Pastor Aaron and the elders felt like they had just entered their first year of university, marriage, or military service. It was a brand new, exciting world of learning and growing. Thankfully, they also had confidence that they were doing the right thing as they entered the intensity of training camp.

THE LOCAL CHURCH IN THE SENDING OF MISSIONARIES

The biblical theology of the local church's sending role can be developed in several different ways. In this chapter, we've chosen to focus on the New Testament use of the word *propempo* (προπέμπω). Over the course of development in the first century, from Acts to 3 John, the term became increasingly specific to local churches that sent out gospel workers.

PROPEMPO IN THE NEW TESTAMENT

First, let's examine the term *propempo* and its occurrences in the New Testament. *Propempo*, as we have seen, literally means "to send forward or to send ahead." It also can mean "to accompany or fully equip for a journey." Second, we'll note other significant missions-sending precedents in the early church. Finally, we'll think through some applications for missions today.

Let's walk through the biblical occurrences of *propempo* together, starting with Acts 15:3: "So, being sent on their way by the church, they passed through both Phoenicia and Samaria, describing in detail the conversion of the Gentiles, and brought great joy to all the brothers."

This verse lies in the middle of a very important scene. Acts 15 tells the story of the early church's Jerusalem Council in which leaders—the Apostles, the elders from Jerusalem, and those sent down from the church in Antioch—came together to decide whether or not the Gentiles needed to follow Jewish ceremonial law to become believers (i.e., to become Christians). This was a crucial, historic decision for the early church.

Paul and Barnabas had returned from their first missionary trip, where they discovered that people were being saved completely apart from Jewish law. Gentiles were getting saved. Jews were getting saved. And the conversion of those people had nothing to do with compliance with Jewish law. So, Paul and Barnabas were the perfect emissaries and spokesmen for the cause of salvation by grace through faith alone. They were selected and commissioned by the church and given authority to represent their case. Then they were sent on their way (*propempo*-ed, so to speak) by the church. The situation also implies that they received whatever they needed for their trip—travel expenses, including expenses for food and accommodations—so that they could do whatever tasks the church had appointed them to do.

After they had ministered in various cities, Acts 20:37–38 describes a farewell scene: "And there was much weeping on the part of all; they embraced Paul and kissed him, being sorrowful most of all because of the word he had spoken, that they would not see his face again. And they accompanied him to the ship." Here, Paul spoke to the Ephesian elders and others from the church he had planted. He was taking leave of them, returning to Jerusalem. These dear people, who loved Paul for his ministry to them, were sorrowful. They accompanied (*propempo*-ed) him to the ship. The tone also implies that they were participating with him in his intended task. They encouraged him along the way. So he went on his way toward Jerusalem.

Paul continued on his way to Jerusalem. He visited with believers along the way. Ships in those days would make multiple stops across a long-distance journey for various reasons. The dear believers of Tyre accompanied Paul's entourage to the boat. Acts 21:5 reads, "When our days there were ended, we departed and went on our journey, and they all, with wives and children, accompanied us until we were outside the city. And kneeling down on the beach, we prayed." "Accompanied them" is another translation of *propempo*. Luke's use of "we" and "us" indicates that he was part of the group traveling together. This scene is a picture of their solidarity and partnership. It almost certainly included some material supply for the ongoing journey.

Another occurrence of *propempo* comes near the conclusion of the fantastic Book of Romans. Romans 15:24 states: "I hope to see you in passing as I go to Spain, and to be helped on my journey there by you, once I have enjoyed your company for a while." Paul is writing to the local church in Rome, and he expects them to fulfill this request "to be helped on my journey there by you." That's the *propempo* phrase. We see it as a specific partnership with the view of sending someone out to a place where the gospel hasn't gone previously—to an unreached people group, as it were. In fact, Paul explains earlier in this chapter that he has proclaimed the gospel in many other places around the Mediterranean. Now, he wanted to go to Spain to take the gospel there. This context implies that people from the church in Rome would accompany him. Paul suggests they share as partners, helping fund his missionary goals and sending qualified teammates along for that ministry.

Next, 1 Corinthians 16:5–6 offers an even more expansive use of *propempo*: "I will visit you after passing through Macedonia, for I intend to pass through Macedonia, and perhaps I will stay with you or even spend the winter, so that you may help me on my journey, wherever I go." This occurrence of *propempo* is translated as "help me on my journey." It certainly implies material supply to do the work of the ministry. "Wherever I go" suggests that this support is not specific to a place. It is a relationship between the missionary and the proposed ministry. Paul expects the church to embrace him, support him, encourage him, and partner with him in the ministry, wherever it is, whatever plans he has.

Paul mentions Timothy in verses 10 and 11 a little further in the text. As 1 Corinthians 16:10–11 reads, "When Timothy comes, see that you put him at ease among you, for he is doing the work of the Lord, as I am. So let no one despise him. Help him on his way in peace, that he may return to me, for I am expecting him with the brothers." This verse provides yet another occurrence of *propempo*, here translated as "help him on his way." The context is of a faithful minister, a disciple, a partner, and an apostolic legate of Paul who will be at their church. Paul says, in effect, "Make sure you take care of him." The request is for material supplies to help Timothy do whatever he is charged to do in his missionary ministry.

Paul's second letter to the Corinthians continues the theme. Second Corinthians 1:16 states: "I wanted to visit you on my way to Macedonia, and to come back to you from Macedonia and have you send me on my way to Judea." The verb in "have you send me on my way" is *propempo*. The thought in this instance is that Paul will visit the church. He is going to stay for some unspecified duration and fellowship with them. He may teach and counsel them for a while. As he moves on, he expects them to participate in sending him on his way, *propempo*-ing him to the next place of ministry. As he mentions in 1 Corinthians and later in 2 Corinthians, the believers in Macedonia (including the Philippian church) have done this all along, consistently supporting, helping, and praying for Paul in his ministry. These local churches participated with a *propempo* perspective in sending out missionaries from their midst.

The next occurrence is in Titus 3:13, which is part of Paul's closing words of his pastoral epistle: "Do your best to speed Zenas the lawyer and Apollos on their way; see that they lack nothing." "Speed... on their way" is the *propempo* phrase. Paul sharpens the intent of his instruction by specifying "that they lack nothing." By this time, *propempo* has developed from its original use across more than twenty years. Here we see *propempo* applied to known, qualified ministers who have delegated authority from a local church or churches to fulfill some specific ministry purpose. It includes the supply of whatever the appointed missionary needs, not only for the journey but presumably for whatever support they need. Now, we have a much fuller understanding of *propempo*. The local church understands that they are supposed to do whatever it takes to help these trusted servants of the gospel achieve their goals in ministry.

The last occurrence is in the little epistle of 3 John, which the Apostle John wrote to a known local church leader, Gaius. Third John 5–8 states:

> Beloved, it is a faithful thing you do in all your efforts for these brothers, strangers as they are, who testified to your love before the church. You will do well to send them on their journey in a manner worthy of God. For

they have gone out for the sake of the name, accepting nothing from the Gentiles. Therefore we ought to support people like these, that we may be fellow workers for the truth.

The *propempo* phrase is here in verse 6 ("send them on their journey"). We see clearly that the church is to care for them, provide hospitality, support them financially and in prayer, and enable them to do their ministry.

This occurrence is perhaps twenty years beyond Paul's writings. *Propempo* has developed from a simple term of assistance and affection to one of ownership and partnership. This development in the use of the term *propempo* was not accidental! The result of knowing servants well in the context of a local church, observing them in ministry, and learning their character, conviction, and competencies lends weight and validation to sending them out into missions ministry.

The biblical theology of supporting and sending out missionaries from the local church, accountable to the local church, develops in the New Testament over a period of more than forty years. During the span of time between Acts 15 and 3 John—respectively, the first and last uses of *propempo*—the concept of sending by the local church takes form. The word becomes increasingly technical in its use. *Propempo* captures the essence of the local church's responsibility to send out workers to areas lacking gospel witness.

As we survey the application of *propempo* in the local churches of the New Testament, we see a number of precedents that reinforce a local-church-centric approach to missions.

MISSIONARIES COME FROM LOCAL CHURCHES

New Testament missionaries arose from a local church context. Missionary candidates weren't just volunteers jetting off on their own or independently joining a parachurch organization to forward their personal "calling" apart from the local church. Qualified missionaries were sent by their local church, which commissioned them to go out.

In Paul's mind, the ultimate goal was reproducing indigenous local churches, which he viewed as the fruit of their work together. The Apostle John appealed to a church leader, Gaius, to continue his church's good work of lavishly loving and providing for the needs of gospel workers. This responsibility was a privilege and duty of the local church body as partners in the truth with these missionaries.

REACHING "NATIONS" AS A THEME IN ACTS

The early chapters in Acts record God-directed outreach, gospel proclamation, and church planting reaching from Jerusalem to other "nations":

- Acts 2 contains a list of around fifteen different foreign-language-speaking ethnicities present at the inauguration of the New Testament church at the Pentecost event.
- Tensions between Hebrew and Hellenist believers are resolved in Acts 6.
- The persecution of the church scattered believers out of Jerusalem and into the regions of Judea and Samaria in Acts 8.
- We see the beginning and affirmation of a new church in Samaria in Acts 8.

- We read of Philip's evangelistic encounter with the Ethiopian in Acts 8, followed by his move to the Mediterranean coast to settle in Caesarea.
- Acts 9 contains the record of the church's growth to Damascus and throughout Judea, Galilee, and Samaria.
- Peter extends the gospel's reach to Lydda, Joppa, and the Gentile audience in the home of the centurion in Caesarea in Acts 9 and 10.
- The expansion of the church and confirmation of its function and fidelity in Antioch of Syria is seen in Acts 11.
- Paul and Barnabas, along with their assistant Mark (also referred to as John Mark), are sent off as missionaries from Antioch to traverse Cyprus, then on to Antioch of Pisidia and points north, in Acts 13 and 14.
- Paul and Barnabas split into two teams, taking Silas and Mark, respectively, as missionaries to their fields of ministry in Acts 15 and 16. Presumably, the sending church at Antioch endorsed both teams.
- Timothy is identified, conscripted, and commissioned from the churches in Galatia to assist Paul and his missionary team in Acts 16. The team also expands to include Luke in Acts 16.

MISSIONARIES ARE QUALIFIED AND AFFIRMED BY THE LOCAL CHURCH

The usual pattern in the New Testament is that the local church validates and approves workers set aside for ministry. This pattern was how the church recognized leaders inside the church fellowship and those sent out for the sake of missions ministry. This was certainly true in the cases of Paul, Barnabas, Silas, Timothy, Titus, and others. Their local church said, "Yes, this person is qualified to go out. This person seems good to join the missionary team." The local church validated and approved workers set aside for ministry. The local church did this when they chose elders and deacons for the church. This occurs officially with the proto-deacons in Acts 6.

This congregational recognition is implemented in the latter half of Acts and throughout the epistles. The qualifications for church leaders are codified in 1 Timothy 3 and Titus 1. They publicly recognize men who have fulfilled the qualifications of spiritual character, conviction, and competencies for ministry, setting them apart as leaders in the church. Should today's missionaries be known, qualified in the context of their local church, and affirmed by the congregation any differently?

SUMMARY OF THE BIBLICAL CASE FOR THE LOCAL CHURCH'S ROLE IN MISSIONS

Think about what we've seen together from the Scriptures:

- Christ loves the local church. He instructed His disciples and Paul about the operation of the local church. He commands His followers to proclaim the gospel, disciple believers in the context of local churches, and go to every ethnic group of humanity to repeat the process.

- The Great Commission cannot be fulfilled apart from indigenous local church members meeting regularly and growing in spiritual maturity. As a natural result of obedience and

- the overflow of the desire to exalt Christ, those churches are to send some of their own to propagate other churches until a church exists in every nation.

- These concepts are what the earliest churches understood from the Lord and obeyed.

- The New Testament and early church history verify these principles, presuming the local church to be the nexus of the practice of Christian life and maturity.

- Paul is the most prominent example of these things, from his personal ministry development to his inspired teaching and writings all the way to the end of his life. Paul personally exemplifies the *propempo* perspective in his view of the local church and its role in missions.

- God the Father's big picture, especially in Ephesians 3, shows the special place reserved for the church in His purposes to display His glory.

- Tracing the term *propempo* illustrates the growing technical sense of the role of the local church in sending servants. The *propempo* perspective illustrates the centrality of the local church in its role of supporting, sending, and shepherding missionaries.

THE GROWING TREND OF LOCAL CHURCH ENGAGEMENT

We are thankful that an increasing number of missionaries and agencies realize that the local church must have a much more significant and substantial role in missions than has usually been the case. In general, this trend is growing. Local churches are stepping up and asking missions-sending agencies to give them more of a role in the sending process, beginning with the original application process. After all, when a potential candidate first tells their church they feel led to pursue missions ministry, their church may not even know them well enough to commend them with integrity.

Agencies are discovering that if they want their missionaries to last a long time in the field, their candidates must be vetted well and validated by their local church. That means the missionary candidate needs to spend time in the local church, demonstrating their ministry, proving their character, and gaining spiritual maturity while realizing there's no quick solution to qualification. Part of the solution to the problem of uncontrolled, preventable attrition from the field is a deep partnership relationship with the sending church.

It is time to roll up our sleeves! The local church must get to work in preparing people for ministry. It takes effort to walk alongside a missionary candidate, helping them to meet the qualifications listed in 1 Timothy 3 and Titus 1. It takes personal attention to ensure a candidate is mature enough to feed themselves spiritually within a foreign, and perhaps hostile, environment. Are they skilled and sufficiently experienced to communicate the gospel and differentiate theological issues within another culture? All churches and agencies need those kinds of workers to establish quality, healthy, biblical churches that are able to reproduce similar indigenous churches.

THE INTENSITY OF TRAINING CAMP

The elders at Hopewell realized that doing their job to equip, train, and send out Kevin and Melissa Langford would be no small undertaking. The elders had to be unified in this effort. A lot of good, enthusiastic communication would be needed at all levels. They had to marshal the whole congregation to be involved in the process. Naturally, their people would have a lot of questions.

If congregational ownership wasn't enough of a challenge, the Langfords' hearts felt the weight of training camp intensity, as they realized all the preparation they were expected to fulfill. The camp's missionary-training curriculum (see appendix B) was not as simple as going through a short orientation course with a bundle of academic classroom teachings on culture shock, language learning, and fundraising. Becoming well equipped to be sent from the church as a missionary for the long haul among an unreached people group takes time, determination, and hard work. Biblical and practical qualifications run the gamut of being, knowing, and doing. Many refer to these major areas as heart, head, and hands—or character, conviction, and competencies.

Vernon Tennant ("Uncle Vernon"), one of the elders at Hopewell, and his wife, Sara, eagerly accepted the role as mentors for Kevin and Melissa Langford. Their primary role would be as accountability and prayer partners for their prefield preparation. The Tennants would serve as sounding boards, cheerleaders, counselors, and coaches to encourage the Langfords toward the finish line.

Pastor Aaron was surprised at the joy and eagerness of the whole congregation in coming together around the grand launch of one of their own into the missions field. Some said they had been praying and hoping for this for a long time! They embraced the new insights from Pastor Aaron's series on the local church's role in missions. There were still questions about the specifics and timing. But together, they trusted God and worked toward solving those questions, which included:

- How long will the whole process take?
- Where will we find the resources to do this extensive training and preparation?
- Where in the world will the Langfords end up serving as missionaries? What people group? What kind of ministry?
- What missions agency will be Hopewell Bible Church's partner and facilitator?
- Can we actually do this?

Congregational ownership of missionary sending is a marathon, not a sprint. There are a lot of moving parts. Thankfully, the Langfords, with the church's help, could accomplish many of the elements of training and preparation simultaneously. Other parts are sequential. Though the beginning is like a training camp, it might feel more complex once you enter the sending process, as if you are creating a multi-specialty team to launch an astronaut into space. In the case of HBC, there were so many things to think about. The question here related to:

- Rocket design: What threshold information and technologies will be optimal to get the Langfords to the field?

- Astronaut readiness: How much strength of body, mind, and will are needed? What training and skills are required to endure the stresses of living in a completely different language and culture? How can we help them prepare for the unknown or unthinkable?

- Tracking and administrative oversight: How will we communicate with them with security in mind? How can we know how they are coping and adjusting? How can we encourage and guide them in their foreign environment and measure their progress toward the purpose and intended goals of the endeavor?

- Specialized environment and vocabulary: What do we and they need to know to navigate entry to a new country, a new social and legal system, and a new range of specialized vocabulary and skills?

The congregation was now wrestling with the realization of having ownership in sending their people to a whole new world for the sake of the gospel. Hopewell Bible Church had a fresh vision for missions. It was their mission, their vision, and their God-given responsibility to launch their own people to do their part in fulfilling the Great Commission.

PART 2

SECURING THE LOCAL CHURCH'S ROLE IN MISSIONS

INTRODUCTION TO PART 2

RESTORE LOCAL CHURCH MISSIONS PHILOSOPHY

In part 2, we move from biblical reflection to application within the local church. The practical and time-tested principles presented here will build a culture of world missions in a local church.

The theme of restoring missions in the local church arises from the gap between biblical ideals and the prevailing practices among evangelical churches today. The overall missions enterprise has gravitated away from local church initiative, input, and involvement.

Our biblical understanding of the centrality of the local church in missions points to the end result of missions being local churches. We take the gospel to all nations in order to establish healthy indigenous local churches. Matthew 28's expression of Christ's mandate indicates this purpose. This goal should shape and influence all the means, strategies, and methodologies used to accomplish Jesus' command. The local church is where the vision for missions begins. Local church leaders must lead their churches by teaching, equipping, and facilitating these ideals. Missions will rise or fall on the local church's ownership of missions.

How do we restore missions to its rightful place in local churches everywhere? There must be a change in the underpinnings at the source of missions teaching, training, and sending. Implementing this change will enable us to achieve the effectiveness the Bible points us toward.

Later, in part 3, we think carefully about the key stakeholders and practitioners inside the church to help align their specific roles with these principles. Also, we'll address other entities in the missions enterprise and how they collaborate with the biblical foundation of a local-church-centric missions philosophy.

Though we're using the expression "Restore Local Church Missions Philosophy," another word besides "restore" might more accurately portray the intended meaning: "repatriate." We want to repatriate missions to the local church. Repatriation is the process of returning an item, an asset, or a person to the rightful place of origin. Restoring emphasizes the responsible agent. Repatriating implies that other entities must negotiate, transfer, and secure ownership to the local church.

An ethically healthy trend today is that large museums are returning artifacts on display that were taken away during colonial days, sometimes by force and against the wishes of the people who originally owned them. Public and private heirs of these artifacts are restoring these works of art, sculptures, and historical artifacts to their place of origin.

Repatriation is also true for people who have been displaced from their homeland, either because they are refugees, prisoners of war, or unable to return to their country of citizenship for some other political or legal reason. Repatriation recognizes their original legal citizenship and facilitates returning them to their home country.

This is what needs to happen with missions and the local church. Missions was owned by local churches from the first century forward.

Over time, many inventive, creative, entrepreneurial people created independent parachurch missions agencies (including relatively independent denominational entities) that have slowly pulled the center of gravity away from local churches and into their own orbit. Let's work toward the healthy repatriation of missions to the local church. Together, we can restore missions in the local church.

MISSIONS AGENCIES ARE NEEDED

Please don't misunderstand! We are not stating that the church doesn't want or need missions-sending agencies. Missions agencies exist to facilitate missions sending in such myriad areas as legal compliance (both at home and abroad), immigration, specialty ministries or target demographics, technical services of all kinds, registration and licensing qualifications, and historical relationships with nationals in a particular country, region, or service. We consistently discourage local churches from sending missionaries without a missions agency's services and expertise. As we have suggested, churches tend to overestimate their capacity to, and underestimate the complexity of, sending missionaries directly on their own. Access to Google search results and AI are not substitutes for real-life, field-tested skills, experience, and relationships.

MISSIONS AGENCIES RUN AWAY FROM LOCAL CHURCH ENGAGEMENT

The founding documents of most, if not all, missions agencies actually state, either directly or indirectly, that they were created to serve, assist, or facilitate local churches in their mission. Yet decades after their founding, missions agencies tend to neglect and sometimes consciously resist local church involvement with their missionaries. We've read a report quoting a missions leader saying, "If the Great Commission is up to the local church, we are in trouble. We are *hardening our work* against church failure in the US."[5] *Hardening our work.* This statement betrays a resistance to the local church's role and a reluctance to actively help restore local church missions philosophy. An attempt to justify this attitude reveals a misconception of "church" in the New Testament. Many conversations with missions agency leaders show that they think they are somehow serving the universal church without intending to serve local churches. This is a tragedy!

FIRST STEPS IN RECLAIMING MISSIONS

The first step in the repatriation process is that the church must reclaim its ownership of missions. Those in the corporate missions enterprise must understand that the local church is the rightful heir of missions responsibility, meaning that missions are not the exclusive domain of parachurch organizations.

Returning missions ownership to the local church will take a lot of work. In part 2, we will focus on a handful of fundamental principles essential for the whole church to grasp in order to restore missions in the local church.

OVERVIEW OF PART 2

In "Satisfy Objections to Local Church Engagement in Missions," common objections from inside the church and from missions agencies are met with suggested answers.

"Sharpen the Biblical Goal of Missions" explains how church leaders teach and guide the Missions Team/Committee and the church

---

5. Ted Esler, "Hardening the Agency," *TedQuarters*, October 6, 2023, https://tedesler.substack.com/p/hardening-the-agency. Emphasis is original.

body to clearly understand the biblical goal of missions. Doing so informs the church's vision and definitions, which then answers the questions of who, what, and why regarding church support for missions.

"Select Missionaries from Your Midst" addresses questions like: Do we wait for volunteers to appear? Do we proactively draft likely candidates? How can we grow new missionaries?

Most churches haven't realized that a special missions focus is not only allowable but preferable. We'll explore how and why to develop such a focus in "Search for a Strategic Missions Focus."

In "Specify Your Church's Missions Resources," we suggest a consistent plan for deciding who to support and how much support to give them, and for creating a rationale for both.

"Stimulate Your Congregation for Missions Involvement" makes clear that every member can be a world Christian, though not every Christian is a missionary. Many members can share in various ways beyond the usual financial support and prayer. Giving information, inspiration, and invitations across the spectrum of ministry opportunities builds a growing ownership of involvement from personal evangelism to reaching UPGs with the gospel.

In "Sustain a Missions Culture in Your Church," we discuss how missionaries come forward from a culture of missions involvement. If the church loves and is involved with its missionaries, those relationships and models will be infused in every generation. The church can be encouraged to live and breathe God's heart for the nations in their daily lives.

"Send and Shepherd Your Missionary Well" will help answer questions like: What do we do once we have a missionary candidate? How can our local church engage in the training and preparation of our candidate(s)? Finally, what structure do we need to ensure that our sent ones are cared for, doing well, and committed for the long haul?

Dear reader, if you are not a church or missions leader at your church, take heart! You can prayerfully and humbly work with your pastor and missions leader to help them understand these things. After you first see these principles from the Scriptures, the next step is to think through how to implement them in your church. That is our prayer. That is the direction we're going in part 2.

GETTING READY FOR LAUNCH

The church was getting ready. Kevin and Melissa Langford were getting prepared. The elders were involved. Uncle Vernon and Sara Tennant were mentoring the Langfords. Kevin was on track to become qualified to serve as an elder, using Hopewell's elder training process and 1 Timothy 3 and Titus 1 as the standard. Slow and steady wins the race!

It had been two years since the initial seed-thought about the Langfords becoming missionaries came to Hopewell Bible Church. Initially, it took a while for the church to get up to highway speed from the initial on-ramp of the idea and vision. But a lot had now been accomplished! Things like:

- Kevin and Melissa Langford took the core sequence of courses through an online seminary recommended by their

Restore Local Church Missions Philosophy

church to give them a strong foundation in the Bible and theology.

- Chuck Davis, the elder of missions, and the Langfords surveyed the congregation to discover members' connections, relationships, or inclinations concerning unreached people groups as their missions field.

- After finding the best match, Hopewell Bible Church entered into a partnership agreement with a missions-sending organization to facilitate sending their missionaries. The organization provided training sessions to equip Kevin and Melissa for beginning cross-cultural ministry; this included training in field security, personal and spiritual disciplines, and strategic decision-making for their proposed field, among many other topics.

- After resigning from his secular employment to pursue his missions calling, Kevin was recognized as a fully elder-qualified pastoral intern at HBC in order to learn more about the dynamics of church leadership and build a stronger bridge of relational support within the church body.

- Kevin and Melissa had become more and more involved in Hopewell's ministries. They helped teach or lead at every age level of the church. They led or planned ministry events and built strong friendships with the people of HBC.

- The Langfords were aiming for a people group in East Asia. Along with a small supportive team from HBC, they scheduled a field exploratory trip. They planned to evaluate what skills and information were needed before they arrived in the field ready for language learning and to establish a pathway to their intended ministry.

- The Langfords and the church pursued relationships with other missionaries who had experience in their chosen target ministry country to learn the ins and outs of missionary life there. They also identified some people in the large city nearest Hopewell who came from that same target area to learn more about the languages, culture, and social cues.

- The congregation had become more comfortable with their ownership role as a church in sending the Langfords to their missions field. They now had a "Barnabas Team" support group to track along with the Langfords and meet their concerns in the areas of prayer, encouragement, logistics, personal finances, technologies, communication, and security.

Formidable milestones still loomed before the Langfords and Hopewell. This was an excellent time to look ahead in the marathon journey and consider what lay between the Langfords and the finish line of being officially sent out.

8

SATISFY OBJECTIONS TO LOCAL CHURCH ENGAGEMENT IN MISSIONS

Lord willing, after reading part 1, "Seeing the Local Church's Role in Missions from the Word," you are curious about implementation. You may also have questions: What difference does it make practically? What should our church do about it? How does this change what we do? How should we think differently about missions in the local church? Your first question might concern how to address objections from within your church.

ANSWERING REACTION QUESTIONS ABOUT IMPLEMENTATION

We don't usually welcome change. Some will reflexively raise objections. Those objections might be tension-laced, emotional protests. Answering objections to change is never easy, even if the prospective changes are for the right reasons and purposes.

Responding to resistance might be challenging. It can be awkward. Here, we'll show you how to understand and respond to those objections gracefully. We have seen pastors, elders, and regular church members offer their concerns.

Missions-sending agencies might have objections too. They are parachurch, nonprofit organizations. Some of them are denominational missions agencies. While those may not strictly be parachurch, they operate similarly and have similar questions.

After considering the most common objections and how to answer them, we will explain a helpful concept called "grandfathering."

INERTIAL RESISTANCE

Whenever you ask a pastor if their church is missions-minded, they will always answer, "Yes." They are preprogrammed to know that missions is not just a vital part of the local church or a segment; it is one of the indispensable reasons for the existence of the local church. So they always answer, "Yes. We are missions-minded."

When pressed for an explanation, the answer is something like this: "We are missional here." What they mean by this popular term "missional" is that they are outreach-oriented in their location. "We love doing evangelism. We love serving our community." The term "missional" is somehow intended to replace missions.

IS "MISSIONAL" GOOD ENOUGH?

The first dissent is due to a weak understanding of the distinction between "missions" and "missional." Traditionally, missions is defined as cross-cultural missions, taking the gospel where there is little or no access to it. Pastors claim a "missional" exemption by referencing Acts 1:8, Christ's command to be "my witnesses in Jerusalem and in all Judea and Samaria, and to the end of the earth." They say, "See, we have a biblical precedent here because we plan to reach our Jerusalem first. Later, we will go out to our Judea and Samaria, and finally, we'll reach the end of the earth." The problem is that Acts 1:8 is not sequential. It is simultaneous. The words are: "Jerusalem *and* in all Judea *and* Samaria, *and* to the end of the earth." The conjunction means all at the same time. It does not mean locally at first, afterward a little farther away, and finally, to the rest of the planet. Jesus teaches a similar simultaneity: you're never finished reaching the poor among you. You never finish reaching your "Jerusalem." Neither the text nor the context supports a "missional" exemption reading of Acts 1:8. Replacing the term "missions" (having to do with international cross-cultural ministry) with "missional" (used for any outreach) is not supported by the text.

WON'T MAKING MISSIONS A HIGHER PRIORITY REDUCE LOCAL OUTREACH?

Some church leaders have expressed genuine concern that growing a larger interest in missions will reduce interest and resources for the local church's local evangelistic outreach.

They are well meaning when they say, "World missions funding will result in decreased giving for church ministries locally." That fear is unfounded. Church giving and God's resources are not a zero-sum game. There is no fixed limitation on the sum of financial resources in God's economy. It is not as if one ministry getting a larger piece of the pie limits everyone else to smaller pieces of a fixed-sized pie. Evidence from experience usually overcomes the lack of faith and confidence in God's supply. If you properly balance how you promote missions and your vision to reach the world, the Lord will sustain funding for every ministry in the church. There is something dynamically attractive about a grand vision and purpose outside of yourself that attracts resources. Sometimes, additional funding even comes from outside the fearful local church.

This pattern is the testimony of many pastors. Even though they may have been reluctant initially to take a stand for strengthening the church's missions ministries, funding did not become an issue when they ultimately did it. A common maxim in development and funding circles is that "funding follows vision."

In general, the local church will not lack funds for local ministry because of an emphasis or a priority on funding world missions. To be sure, there are a few examples of churches that overemphasize world missions giving to their detriment. They sacrifice baseline priorities such as repairing and upgrading their facilities in order to maintain bragging rights about how much the church gives to missions. Proper priorities in giving to missions are a matter of godly wisdom.

BUT WE WEREN'T TAUGHT THIS IN SEMINARY!

Several pastors have individually told us, "I don't think we can do this because I never learned about this in seminary." There are multiple issues with this argument. There are many reasons why they didn't learn about the local church's biblical role in missions. The typical Bible school or seminary's MDiv curriculum reveals a weak spot on this issue. Given the dominance of missions agencies in Western missions, it's no wonder that ministry training institutions assume the local church plays an inferior role. So, it's probably true that the pastor never learned the proper biblical view of the local church in missions. Many have never studied or come in contact with the concept of the centrality of the local church in missions.

Further, because of this unintentional deficit, they have never learned how to lead in that direction or build the organization and practice of foreign missions as a significant church ministry. The senior pastor leading his church in missions should be part of Practical Ecclesiology 101. By God's grace, the teachable pastor will learn and become an effective champion for the local church's role in missions.

OUR CHURCH MIGHT LOSE OUR BEST AND BRIGHTEST

Ardent pastors, zealous for raising up ministry leaders in their congregation, have expressed fear that sending missionaries might take away their most capable people. Right, that's true. It happened in Antioch. Remember, in Acts 13, Barnabas and Saul were commissioned by the elders and their church to go out in missionary work. Were they the best and brightest of the church? They were undoubtedly very qualified and gifted. They both were instrumental in establishing and planting the church in Antioch.

So, were they capable people? Yes. Is that a sacrifice? Yes. Is training and sending what the church is supposed to be about? Yes. Training and sending is a normal biblical pattern. The church should be multiplying local churches. Naturally, that means that the church will be sending out church planters. This organic process includes raising and equipping missionaries from within, then sending them out to plant other local churches within every language group worldwide.

TYPICAL AGENCY OBJECTIONS

Now, let's move on to some objections from missions organizations. We've heard it put this way: "Because we are an IRS-approved non-profit organization, we must be able to prove that we are legally and organizationally independent from outside control. Therefore, we're not allowed to partner with churches or share control of our employees and information with an outside entity." They must indeed maintain organizational control to protect the purposes of their charter. However, that doesn't mean nonprofit organizations must keep local sending churches disconnected from the missionaries those churches send out!

There are many things that agencies routinely outsource domestically and internationally. Every missions agency we know outsources significant administrative and human resources duties to third parties. They have outside service providers that utilize confidential personnel information and management. Agencies contract with insurance carriers to provide or underwrite insurance for their missionaries, a process which involves a lot of HIPAA-level information. They often hire outside accountants, auditors, and group retirement fund agents to serve the organization. They contract with other outside agencies for website services, social media promotion, development, and grant-writing services. Internationally, they partner and outsource with international services and individuals to do all kinds of work for them: legal services, immigration, national ministry partnerships, etc.

Thus, it should be no big deal for the missions agency to have partnership agreements with local churches to send their people as missionaries. Here are helpful responses to common objections to such formal partnerships:

> **Objection:** We can't legally allow outsiders access to private personnel records.
>
> **Answer:** The organization already does this when outsourcing financial and HR functions. Also, it is permissible when the employee/member of the organization signs

a release statement to allow access to leaders of the sending church.

Objection: We must legally exercise exclusive and inviolable control over personnel assignments, ministry direction, and team dynamics.

Answer: This objection contradicts the organization's normal flexibility in practice, which allows for field- and corporate-level partnerships, personal preferences, and the discretion of the missionary or team. In the field, the agency responds dynamically to many factors. There is no legal reason why it and its personnel could not agree to input from a dynamic partnership with the sending church.

THE SENDING CHURCH KNOWS ITS MISSIONARY BEST!

Not only is a local church partnership possible, but it is also important because the local church knows its missionary best. The sending church can best enter into the shepherding and care, or what missions agencies call "member care." When allowed and equipped to do so, the sending church can marshal ongoing, personalized care and resources for their people better than the missions agency. The missions agency often shows up for intervention care only after a crisis has erupted. The sending church shows up every day, every week, and every month before a crisis can even surface.

We've mentioned it previously, and we know from experience that this is generally true: if missions agencies partnered with local churches in substantive ways in caring for their missionaries, then the missionary attrition rate for preventable causes would drop precipitously.

When this partnership is mutually agreed upon and fostered, it yields notable positive results for the individuals involved and fosters the long-term stability and health of the missionary, thereby increasing the fruitfulness of the missions work.

In all candor, there have been cases in which the insertion of the sending church into a crisis proved detrimental to the overall situation in the field. However, in those cases:

- The missions agency informed the sending church after the situation had already escalated to a level requiring intervention.
- The sending church had not communicated frequently and transparently enough with their missionary to anticipate the gravity of the problem.
- The sending church wrongfully assumed that their sent one was in the right and all others were in the wrong. In the heat of the crisis, they did not seek or give credit to perspectives from others who were affected, insisting on a solution that satisfied their sent one at the cost of more harm to or attrition in the field.

MISSIONS AGENCIES HAVE AN EXCLUSIVE ADVANTAGE

In objecting to increasing their involvement with local sending churches, missions organizations sometimes tell us, "We know how to do missions in the field. Churches don't." There is some truth to that.

Why don't churches know how to do this? Broadly, it's because they haven't been allowed to do this. It's like saying, "My fifteen-year-old doesn't know how to drive." That's probably because they have not been allowed to drive yet. What do you do with a fifteen-year-old who wants to learn to drive? You spend a lot of time teaching them how to drive. The student driver has to learn how to operate the pedals, steering wheel, control knobs, buttons, stalks, mirrors, and levers in the car. They've got to develop situational awareness as a driver. They have to learn the laws and practical rules of the road. You teach him or her all the skills necessary to drive safely and alertly in order to avoid accidents and get from point A to point B. So, you take the time to coach and supervise them as they change the tires; you teach them repeatedly how to use the turn signals, look both ways for traffic, etc. In time, they do these things easily. The parents get relief from not having to do all the driving themselves!

The process of learning new skills isn't rocket science. Churches can learn how to shepherd their missionary. Churches can understand the nuances of the prevailing culture, field ministry, team dynamics, and field stressors. The missions agencies must allow them to learn these things and then to do them. In fact, missions agencies would ideally insist that local sending churches do these things for their missionaries.

It doesn't mean that the local churches have to do everything. However, the things that local churches are best at doing and need to be most involved in concern the ministry direction and shepherding of their people. They should be encouraged to embrace those responsibilities. Thoughtful churches are usually better than the missions agency in these areas.

BUT AREN'T FIELD ISSUES TOO COMPLEX FOR A LOCAL CHURCH?

It's sad but true. We've heard missions agency leaders say, "Churches are incapable of understanding missions issues and ministry vision on a foreign field." The solution to this objection is just like the previous one. Give them a chance. Help them see the information. Help them get in touch with people who know the issues of strategy and vision in the field. In general, sincere, engaged local churches will love it and do an outstanding job when given the opportunity.

> **Objection:** The local church doesn't understand the complexity of caring for missionaries in situations of severe cross-cultural stress.
>
> **Answer:** The sending church knows, loves, and has a lifelong commitment to their members, whether they are missionaries or not. Churches are not incapable of learning those complexities. Good shepherding of their people is one of the things that good sending churches do best. Missionaries who have a great relationship with their sending church are the envy of other missionaries in their field who do not have such a relationship. (See attrition information in chapter 15.)

IT'S MORE ECONOMICAL TO LET THE AGENCY DO IT, RIGHT?

Another objection of missions agencies is very straightforward: "We are much more efficient than the local church." That statement might be true in raw financial terms. However, we would still respond with, "Show us the numbers." We know of denominational agencies that spend 40 percent of all income on things other than field ministry. What we're asking churches to do is mostly volunteer work in comparison to agency staffing and expenses. It costs the missions agency nothing. It costs the local church something, but they're willing to do it out of love for their sent one and ownership of the ministry in the field. If missions agencies allowed local sending churches to be involved, at least some agency overhead costs would go down.

There are a lot of things that missions agencies do better than churches. They can provide group insurance, retirement policies, and relationships with nationals and local service organizations to help their sent ones get the job done. Many things are essential to the administration of organizational structure. Let the agencies do what they do best and then partner with sending churches to enable them to do what the sending church does better.

PRACTICAL APPLICATION OF "GRANDFATHERING"

Now, we come to this last concept to help us sort out exceptions and objections. "Grandfathering" is a legal expression. It means exempting a preexisting status from a new rule, law, or regulation. One type of resistance we hear is, "It's too hard to turn the battleship of our missions organization/church to embrace a more local-church-centric philosophy of doing missions."

You'll never turn the battleship if you never decide to turn the rudder. You've got to make a change. You've got to commit and say, "This is our preferred future." Grandfathering means you can exempt everything that exists presently. Just because you're taking a turn for the better doesn't mean you have to immediately wipe out everything that doesn't fit the preferred future.

If we are to restore missions in the local church, we will have to manage some change. We look to a better future and define what that should be. We grandfather everything that exists now, at least for a while. We work steadily toward the desired ideal over two, three, and five years. At the finish line, all of the grandfathered people, policies, and practices recede into the background of the past. Things that don't fit the new paradigm will graciously retire, expire, or be released.

Implementing your new paradigm must be thoughtful, intentional, and well communicated. The new way of doing things takes root in the field, the home office, and the local church as it unfolds. There may be initial stress, but not catastrophe. There are many blessings that come after the change! The shift yields satisfaction and results from a firm biblical foundation. We contend that the Bible, the data on attrition, the practical experience, and the funding all push us toward restoring missions in the local church.

Ready, set, go!

MILESTONES TO THE FINISH LINE

The Langfords and the leadership of Hopewell discovered that one of the final milestones they needed to get past involved objections to the level of attention and resources it would take to send the Langfords. Earnest people feared that the excitement about foreign missions would automatically torpedo efforts to evangelize people in their own community. They didn't realize it immediately, but the church actually now had more people excited about sharing Christ with their neighbors and more involvement in local evangelism efforts than ever before.

Others expressed reluctance because, they said, "We've never done it that way before." Most of the adults at Hopewell Bible Church had some experience in other churches that supported missionaries or did missions in various ways. The idea of local-church-centered preparation, sending, and shepherding of missionaries was new. It was all exciting. It seemed biblical. But it was unknown territory. It was a lot to take on.

These objections kept surfacing. So much so that Pastor Aaron, the elders, Kevin Langford, and Melissa Langford had to ask each other regularly, "How's it going? What new problems have popped up?" Their first response was to concede the point: "Of course, we've never done it that way before! We always assumed that it was somebody else's job. Now we know that it is our job. We believe it will be best for everybody involved, including our target people group in East Asia. We have already experienced the positive difference it makes within our church body, our confidence in the preparation of the Langfords, and our sense of true partnership in the Great Commission."

Some of the older members said, "We can't do this." But Hopewell Bible Church was actually engaging and becoming a sending church. By and large, the congregation was putting their shoulder to it and taking on the load of a loving and responsible ownership of the Langfords, their missionary vision, and the work necessary to bring it to reality. With the help of their partner missions agency, the church had identified and fulfilled most of the steps of training and qualifications for being sent as missionaries from their church, with all having reasonable hope of their success in their chosen people group over the long haul. On the other hand, it was true that they themselves couldn't do this. God was doing this. He has told us through His Word that He wants us to do this. He is with us and enables us in it all. God was doing this through Hopewell because it was His command and His will that they do so. They needed to continue to trust Him through to the end. That meant not just until they sent Kevin and Melissa to the field. It meant through their whole work and ministry in the field and through the miraculous result of seeing a church planted in that people group where there had never been one before. That was what they were doing, by God's grace and with His help.

Again, ripples of long-term members said, "What about the dear people we already support? Will we be cutting their support to do this?" Pastor Aaron and the leaders of Hopewell Bible Church knew this concern was coming because they had had those same thoughts. Fortunately, they understood that good communication with their supported missionary partners was to be a part of this process. All missionaries were informed of the exciting new opportunity for Hopewell Bible Church to support one of their couples in going to the field. They were also made aware that the church would evaluate or reevaluate the alignment of those they supported with HBC's clearer vision of a biblical definition of missions, appropriate goals for field ministry, and the need for doctrinal and strategic alignment with the church's missions vision. Between the start of Kevin and Melissa Langford's preparation for the field and sending them to the field with a significant financial commitment from HBC, all the presently supported missionaries would have had time to interview with HBC leadership. Initially, grandfathering them into the new budget would honor all prior support commitments. However, whatever cuts might be needed would be done graciously over time and with good communication.

One of the last big milestones to the finish line was the Langfords' missionary support. HBC leaders and congregation had learned that faith support has been the primary means of support for missionaries since Hudson Taylor and the China Inland Mission in 1865. Jesus was supported like this. Paul was supported like this. The process of raising and sustaining support partners both builds one's character and tests one's qualifications.

SUPPORT-RAISING BECOMES A TEAM SPORT

The Langfords were taught in their prefield training that the typical skills for raising support are parallel to and essential for pioneer church planting. Both involve winsome relationship skills, a commitment to regular communication and follow-up, persuasively presenting intangible truths, and giving opportunities for response. Now, the Langfords gave themselves to diligent communication and prayer for support-raising as they looked forward to their exploratory trip to East Asia. Ed Fontana, HBC's elder of finance, came alongside the Langfords' Barnabas Team and others interested in the congregation to create a communication and presentation plan to contact possible support partners. Pastor Aaron agreed to write letters of introduction to pastors of other churches from their wider fellowship and to friends from his seminary days. This ad hoc team designed and created a packet of information to introduce the Langfords, their planned field ministry, and the church's missions goals. The Langfords ransacked their contacts and Christmas card list to create the foundation of a master address list. Pastor Aaron added his contacts. Friends within HBC added friends and church contacts to the list. They began to think about scheduling and home meetings to follow up. Their first newsletter went out both by email and snail mail. They prayed like crazy for God's provision. The church was already committed to providing 20 percent of the support needed to get them started.

The Barnabas Team (now often tagged the "B-Team") committed to following up on the presentation by making phone calls and booking tentative appointments. Kevin and Melissa shared an online calendar with the B-Team to determine their availability. The Langfords had to cut back on their local church commitments at Hopewell so they could be free to visit other churches, other Missions Teams, and other potential supporters. Their policy was to share their calling and vision. They would also make clear Hopewell's role in sending them and meeting specific financial needs and have some time for Q and A. Then they would simply trust God for His provision.

The people of Hopewell were admirably sharing the burden of sending Kevin and Melissa to the field. They all looked forward to the specifics of the ministry vision becoming clearer when the Langfords arrived in the field.

SHARPEN THE BIBLICAL GOAL OF MISSIONS

We've discussed the biblical basis for the centrality of the local church in missions. Now, we are moving into concepts for practical implementation in the local church. What are some significant ideas to help us apply renewed biblical vision and conviction about the local church's role in missions?

One key to repatriating and securing the church's role is to sharpen the biblical goal of missions. We need to clarify what we mean by missions, what the goal of missions is, and how we arrive at that goal. This consideration has several facets. We won't be able to cover them entirely. Hopefully, the discussion will arouse your interest and inform your thoughts about applications to your church.

You might think that clarifying the goal of missions would be easy. That's not the case. Even after reviewing the biblical view of the church, as we have, people retain all kinds of preconceived ideas about what missions is. Even pastors and missions leaders have preformed ideas, some shaped by traditions and cultures, some by modern influences.

They may think they are adequately informed by the contemporary streams of thought on missions, so it takes humility to go back to the Bible to find out what missions was all about for those first-century Christians through the example of the Apostles and the original writers of the New Testament.

KEEPING THE MAIN THING THE MAIN THING

The bottom line is this: the biblical goal of missions is the local church. If you want to sharpen the goal of missions, the answer is the local church. What is God's purpose? His glory. By what means does He achieve it? Through the local church. We see this over and over again in the New Testament.

How does God fulfill His glory through the local church? There are a lot of dimensions to that. God wants to build in us a holy life. He wants us to worship Him. Those two outcomes are best achieved in heaven. So, what remains?

He wants the church to demonstrate the gospel and testify to Jesus Christ. Evangelism, discipleship, and missions are done here and now. We see through the letters of the New Testament that the main thing that God uses is the body of Christ. Mutually committed disciples grow in spiritual maturity together as they learn to obey the Scriptures. An unconnected believer cannot do that alone; spiritual maturity comes from relationships in the local church.

It's not all about Sunday morning preaching. It's not about Sunday school, small groups, or the equivalent. It's not just about Bible studies. It is about the interaction and practical application of biblical truth to natural, human, and saved sinners like us. Dynamic life within the local church smooths our rough edges as we grow together in Christ and truth. That's Ephesians 4. We interact with God's Word and apply it to our hearts and behavior to obey and follow it throughout the nitty-gritty of real life. Doing so is a testimony to all those who watch us from outside. As the church grows in maturity, influence, and outreach, that dynamism is extended to other local churches. Whenever a church is involved in planting a new local church, we reinforce, develop, encourage, and strengthen believers to advance the testimony of Christ for the glory of God.

CLARIFY YOUR GOAL OF MISSIONS

To build missions in and through the local church, we must clarify the goal of missions. It relates to church planting or establishing churches outside of one's church. Many things are necessary in the process of developing another church:

- **The Bible:** There must be a Bible (at least the New Testament) accessible and understandable in the people's language. Translators and missionaries may debate whether or not a particular dialect translation is necessary if a majority language, related dialect, or trade language translation is already accessible. We will not solve that dilemma here. The point is that the Bible is the inspired Word of God. The Bible is how we know Christ and the gospel. It is critical to saving faith. The Scripture alone is our final authority for faith and practice.

- **A target audience:** This has a "sending" and "going" factor. Usually, a local church sends a person, family, or team to a particular target destination to plant a church there. It might be local, across town. It might be domestic, cross-cultural, cross-state, or countrywide. It might be international. For our purposes, "missions" implies international cross-cultural ministry.

- **A messenger:** There must be someone qualified and committed to proclaim and teach Christ from the Scriptures.

- **A plurality of leaders:** A leadership team emerges as the church develops (if the church was not started initially with a leadership team). A vital part of the goal is to raise and train leaders for the new church. A biblically qualified plurality of indigenous elders is the standard. Installing indigenous leaders is a natural development and the New Testament presumption for church leadership.

CLARIFY THE DEFINITION OF THE LOCAL CHURCH

If the goal is planting and strengthening local churches, what are the essential ingredients of a local church? What are the biblical basics of a local church? The definition of a local church, as implied by the Great Commission texts, includes these elements:

- It consists of a mutually committed body of local believers.
- They worship regularly together.
- They teach the Word of God and practice prayer.
- They are under the leadership of biblically qualified shepherds.
- They actively share the gospel in their circle of influence.

It might be helpful to note elements that are *not* in this definition of the local church. There are no requirements related to:

- paid staff
- a building dedicated solely to the church's use
- anything electronic
- a particular style of music
- other structured ministry programs

HOW DOES THIS FOCUS REFINE MISSIONS MINISTRIES?

All missions should aim to establish local churches and equip local church leaders to do the same in every nation, tongue, tribe, and ethnicity worldwide. So, you may ask, "How does this play out in our church missions ministries?"

Many people who think of modern missionary work think of solutions to desperate needs around the world, including things like:

- well drilling and potable water supply projects
- medical, dental, and primary health care clinics
- prevention of human trafficking
- sports evangelism
- mass evangelism meetings
- community development and poverty alleviation
- AIDS-related programs
- translation of Christian books
- agricultural and reforestation development
- internet evangelism
- teaching English

- computer or IT training
- electrical supply projects
- youth ministries and camps
- disaster relief
- and more!

Yet the most remarkable human need is for the gospel. For example, people who are concerned about issues of social justice and human trafficking have to deal with the fact that it seems like a more profound injustice for people never to have a chance to hear the gospel. As Christians, even simply as humans, we should be appalled by the deplorable circumstances and injustices that evidence a fallen world. Human needs grip us. Sometimes, life and death hang in the balance. The spiritually lost may need to be rescued from death in order even to have a chance to hear the gospel; but too often, we confuse means with ends. We mix up strategies with results. Our desire for holistic transformation of life and society can eclipse the clear biblical priority of proclamation of the gospel.

Missions strategies that do not intentionally start, sustain, and multiply indigenous local churches fall short of the biblical ideal. Projects that began as an entry point in the community to share the gospel can quickly become a distraction. They can so consume resources and staffing that the means never attain the end. Instead, the means become the end.

Disciple-making is the core of the Great Commission. Great Commission–driven disciple-making will naturally result in local churches. Churches embody "discipling, baptizing, and teaching all I commanded you" in a mutually committed worshiping body of believers. Planting local churches is clearly what the first-century believers understood and did. Those modern missionary ministry solutions listed earlier can be good and legitimate means to create indigenous local churches. Those strategies should ultimately build bridges, establish relationships, and open up opportunities to facilitate the goal of planting churches.

Indigenous local churches are the God-ordained instruments for each people group to reach and disciple its own people group. Local churches should insist that their missionaries have a conscious, intentional goal of strengthening and planting local churches through whatever ministry they have. It is OK to ask, "How will your ministry link into the chain that leads to new and strong local churches?"

AN EXAMPLE OF SHARPENING FOCUS IN A "MISSIONS" MINISTRY

A typical example of this concern is seen when churches support local college student ministries. The people involved in that ministry should bring the fruit of their campus evangelism and discipleship into strong, healthy local churches. That doesn't mean they form a church of their own on campus. A so-called "campus church" is not a church unless it exhibits all the characteristics of a church—that is, unless it is open to people from all age groups, has biblically qualified leaders, observes the ordinances of the church, etc.

However, those campus ministries can disciple students, lead them, and show them how to become active members in healthy local churches around the university's community. If the campus ministry staff are not doing that, they fall short of fulfilling the Great Commission. Whether it's a sports ministry, service ministry of any kind, relief and development ministry, or evangelism ministry, that ministry should be a stepping stone toward membership in good churches where they can continue to grow all their lives. It is OK to ask, "Does your ministry have clear spiritual goals that make it different from a secular organization doing similar things?"

Similarly, cross-cultural ministries should be linked with a church planting effort or appropriate healthy churches in the field. There should be some linkage with indigenous believers. Then, as there is fruit from the missions ministry, those new disciples can become part of establishing and strengthening local churches. That's where the action is to promote their spiritual maturity for the rest of their lives.

CATALYZING ALIGNMENT TOWARD LOCAL CHURCH GOALS

Any valid ministry can be intentionally linked to seeing local indigenous churches raised and strengthened wherever they are. Sadly, there are a lot of ministries that are not so connected. Campus ministry staff must be asked, "So, this is what you're doing; this is your activity; this is your ministry in the field. What are the results? What are you doing after a person comes to faith in Christ? How are you integrating that person into a healthy local church where they will grow, form relationships, and worship with others like them?"

Some missionaries and missions organizations might say, "We just do our niche. This little bit is what we do; we do it well, and we leave the rest to others." Such thinking needs to be more realistic and aligned with the biblical goal of missions. Does doing so take extra work? Does it take added responsibility and effort for the relationships involved? Yes, it does. But it's worth it in order to pass the fruit of that ministry into good hands. Local church leaders will follow up with those new contacts and new baby Christians to encourage, strengthen, and bring those new believers to maturity.

The following question is a watershed one for restoring missions in the local church. Church leaders should ask this question of every missionary: "In what way do you fulfill the goal of seeing churches planted and strengthened in the context in which you are working?" Regardless of the means, missions must be aimed at the proper end, not making the means an end.

It is incredibly freeing and focusing for the missionary to have this sharpened mindset. Missionaries can pursue their ministry niche when they are focused on the right end goal. Missionaries will have so much more fulfillment than if they followed a course of, say, sending so many kids through youth camp, sports ministry, or whatever and having a certain number of them become believers by saying a prayer, signing a card, or whatever they were invited to do—but then dropping them off, leaving, and going somewhere else.

It is wonderful to know that there is a bigger goal in mind. It involves planting and strengthening the church. There is a comforting assurance of ongoing follow-up and continuing discipleship of individuals and families by worshipers in their community who are reaching their community. Part of the goal is to become independent of foreign missionaries in the future. The believers in the local church are growing and maturing in their faith, stronger in their witness. They become motivated and capable of independently planting and multiplying churches in their people.

Sharpening the goal of missions helps the local church and missions ministries. The goal of missions is the local church.

SHARPER VISION, YET WITH SHADOWS AHEAD

Kevin and Melissa Langford were excited about their exploratory trip to the country of their chosen field. The partner missions agency approved the trip. They would have people waiting for them at the capital airport. The primary purposes were to:

- make initial observations about
  - » probable future living conditions
  - » a language learning plan for the national language
  - » cultural cues and social mores
  - » costs and budget impact
  - » transition and learning resources within the missionary community, especially their own missions agency
- establish relationships with key people who can assist them practically during their first twelve to twenty-four months in the field
- commit to an initial team within their missions agency
- begin to learn the appropriate greeting and leave-taking language and expectations
- develop awareness and demographic knowledge about the

spiritual needs in-country, especially anything related to their targeted unreached people group

- discuss and get insights on all these observations with fellow members of their church. Three church members would spend ten days of the three weeks with them: their mentors, Uncle Vernon and Sara Tennant, and Greg Harrison, the Missions Team leader.

The travel was fine, just exhausting. After being on a spiritual-emotional high for weeks before departure, they now were feeling crushed by jet lag, the immensity of the differences there, and how serious-to-the-bone their commitment was becoming.

FIELD MISSIONARIES ARE SURPRISED

Within a few days, it became apparent that the field leaders of their missions agency didn't understand the role of the Langfords' sending church in the big picture. The field leader knew there was a partnership agreement with Hopewell Bible Church, but the other missionaries had never heard of something like that continuing to function in the field. They received and treated Kevin and Melissa joyfully as field recruits. Yet they didn't understand what their local sending church had to do with it. In the past, the field ran the show without the involvement of anyone's church. So, the presence of others from HBC was a surprise and felt like an imposition on the missionaries' hospitality. Everyone needed a briefing on how that would work, especially in the long-term view. So, there were several warm conversations across the world with the missions agency's home office and the Hopewell Bible Church leaders. In the end, the field missionaries agreed to make it work. Good attitudes and gracious conversations helped dispel any clouds of doubt.

The exploratory trip was intense for Kevin and Melissa! They had underestimated the complexity and difficulty they would face. Now, reality was sinking in. They had a lot to accomplish. The trip was setting the stage for what would be a challenging lifetime of service for the glory of Christ. They ended up choosing and being chosen to join a team just beginning to form that had a goal of church planting in their same target group. The people on their exploratory trip from their sending church were wise and invaluable. Having extra eyes, ears, and hearts with them helped them sort out their emotions, ask better questions, and keep the long-view goal in mind. Their fellow HBC teammates on the trip would be their best, most sympathetic advocates back at Hopewell.

EXPERIENCE PAYS DIVIDENDS

The Langfords returned with lots of great stories and photos. More importantly, they came back with a better understanding of what it would take in terms of sacrifice, determination, and hard work, by God's grace, to see the vision of a church planted in "their" people group come to pass.

Kevin and Melissa realized things they needed to add to their training before returning to the field to begin language learning in earnest:

- exposure to the process of church planting in their home culture
- tweaking and improving the partnership agreement with the missions agency, then communicating it better to all involved
- developing a more explicit timeline with names, dates, possible national partners for the ministry, immigration hurdles

to pass, and the appropriate tools and appliances needed to set up a fitting home in their target area

They were also very thankful for the help and encouragement of their new missions agency team in the field. The agency team's wisdom, experience, and network of relationships would be a deep well of intangible resources for their ministry. They were going to be so helpful for everything in-country.

Returning home to Hopewell Bible Church, the Langfords had a deeper and sharper vision for their future in missions, yet they saw the shadows of the challenges ahead. They were ready to run this last leg of support-raising, preparation, and communication in order to return to East Asia. They were almost ready for the countdown for liftoff.

SELECT MISSIONARIES FROM YOUR MIDST

A second key concept in securing the local church's role in missions is changing how we think about someone becoming a missionary. The biblical church-centric missions philosophy is very different from the typical way people have come to think about missions. How someone becomes a missionary is part of the change of trajectory. The missions enterprise would benefit by moving from an individualistic and missions-agency-driven model to a more local-church-centered mindset.

VALIDATING A MISSIONARY CALL

From the beginning, church leaders and missionary candidates (and missions agencies) should better understand the missionary call. Thankfully, wisdom does not automatically give authoritative weight to subjective and individualistic statements like:

- "God called me to be a missionary."

- "If I don't go as soon as possible, I will be disobedient."
- "God led me to be a missionary in order to…"

The church doesn't just appoint, empower, and support anyone who says they have a God-given urge to be a pastor, elder, missionary, or fill-in-the-blank. In fact, the more insistent that person is, the more likely they are not qualified for whatever position of authority they desire. The people in authority in the church are those the church knows well. They have sufficient and recognized training and experience, and the proven character, to fulfill the ministry position description. The claim of a missionary call is hollow without the relational and corporate verification of that person's character, conviction, and competence for that ministry.

We've already seen the pattern of the New Testament. That is, the candidate for leadership within the church or being sent out by the church earns the commendation of the church and qualifies before being given the position. Missionaries don't get a pass on that.

Another angle on this principle is that the initiative may come from someone other than the potential candidate. Church leaders select and approach a candidate based on qualifications appropriate to the position. The church leaders recognize, equip, and set apart those willing candidates for that particular ministry. Missionaries may be drafted like Timothy was.

Many things strike fear in the heart of a pastor. One of them is someone coming to him and saying, "I think God is calling me to be a missionary. Now, what do I do? Can you and the church help me become a missionary and send me to the field?" If and when that happens, don't panic. This circumstance should be a cause for celebration. It should be a standard product of a maturing church. Praise the Lord and figure out what you're going to do.

If that scenario hasn't happened in your church in recent history, pray that it will happen. Church leaders and church missions leaders should pray that God, in His gracious providence, will be pleased to raise up missionaries from their midst. It is a special privilege and responsibility to send out your own people to a missions field. There is nothing like the church family getting "skin in the game."

BLAZING THE TRAIL TOWARD MISSIONARY QUALIFICATION

No matter the age, experience, or maturity of the person asking the question, there is a pathway if God wants them to become a missionary and you want them to get to the field. If your church is the sending church, you certainly want to help them become an excellent representative of the gospel, of Jesus Christ, and of your church. People and leaders around the candidate are in a better position to judge the fittedness and readiness of a candidate compared to the usual missionary application process from a missions agency office.

The pathway for qualification as a missionary is very similar to that of a pastor or an elder in your church. Added to this are elements of cross-cultural ministry and the missionary role. One of the keys at the very beginning is to find or develop a proper mentor for this missionary candidate. If a candidate couple is coming to you, then a couple should be assigned as their mentors. An unmarried candidate should have a mature believer of the same gender assigned as the mentor. This assignment connects the church leaders, the Missions Team, and the missionary candidate.

The mentor you choose should be godly, mature in their outlook, and willing to learn about missions alongside their mentee. It is more about asking the right questions than knowing everything about missions or missionary training. It should be someone who will be very patient because it will take considerable time, depending on the starting point.

THE BIG PICTURE OF MINISTRY TRAINING

We understand training as involving three major areas of life. These are very well accepted within the personal development community, not just the Christian community. The first is *being*, the second is *knowing*, and the third is *doing*. We have *The Trellis and the Vine*, by Colin Marshall and Tony Payne, to credit for alliterating those categories in a ministry context.[6] Here is our version of them:

- Character, which includes the idea of calling, is *being*.

- Conviction, which has to do with biblical and theological training, is *knowing*.

- Competence, which is ministry skills and experience, is *doing*.

Before describing these three major areas, consider this analogy for missionary training and preparation: the responsibility of parents to train and educate their children. Biblically, we understand that parents are stewards of their children's development until they leave the home. Believers and unbelievers generally know they are responsible for protecting and guiding their children. Doing so involves training in culturally appropriate behavior, respect for authority, and "eating your vegetables." Education requires reading, writing, oral

---

6. Colin Marshall and Tony Payne, *The Trellis and the Vine: The Ministry Mind-Shift That Changes Everything* (Sydney: Matthias Media, 2009).

communication, conversational skills, literature, history, math, sciences, art, music, and sports.

The problem is that you can't do everything. Parents have to be somewhat selective, employing several personal grids: available time, inclinations and interests (both on the part of the parents and the part of the child/children), opportunities, values, and some degree of excellence. Almost every family chooses resources for educating and developing their children using some overlapping networks: community sports leagues, summer camp, piano, guitar, art, history appreciation outings, homeschool cooperative schools, or online classes. When the child reaches high school, someone has to teach math and science, so we often outsource. Public school, private school, some version of homeschool, special skills training, vocational training, trade school, community college, college or university, graduate school—all of these are possible and reasonable choices. The parents, along with their maturing child, make choices. The parents are responsible. They delegate, co-opt, hire, enlist, enroll, and sign up to enable the entire gamut of education and training required. The parents stay in touch during the process and track the grades, values, testing, and competition events. Lastly, their student graduates from school, gets certified or licensed, and is hired for that first job in their field of study.

Similarly, the church is not required to possess all the education and training necessary to fully equip its candidate to be launched into missionary life. Yet the sending church is responsible for ensuring their candidate is adequately prepared with whatever external resources and training are necessary. The church gets proper information and counsel about the options. It's all done under the watchful, nourishing care of the candidate's church family.

BUILDING CHARACTER QUALIFICATION

So, let's start with the *being* area, which we call character. This is what the person is at the root of their personality.

The candidate may say they have a calling. Fine. You need to test, question, and observe it in action. You will be able to discern it over time. Their calling will become evident as an overarching summary of their personnel file told by those around them. A person's calling is tested through hardship, perhaps opposition, patience, and faithfulness. It can be confirmed and affirmed by the body of the local church.

Second, we attend to the candidate's personal spiritual disciplines. This is no small issue. Most beginning missionary candidates don't really have their act together concerning personal spiritual disciplines. Field missionaries need spiritual nurturing and feeding so that they are not dependent on home-side sources while in the field. They must know how to drink from the well of Christ themselves, understand God's Word, and have good Bible study and prayer habits, among other personal spiritual disciplines.

The third part is interpersonal relationships and relational skills. They should know how to solve conflicts and resolve communication issues in a practical manner.

Then there are elder or deacon qualifications, and depending on their role in the field, they will want to be qualified as an elder according to 1 Timothy 3 and Titus 1, or as a deacon according to 1 Timothy 3 (among other references). You want confidence that the candidate has that kind of sterling, above-reproach character as a Christian and leader.

The last part of calling and character is a reputation for integrity. By that, we mean having the same character throughout all the elements of their reputation: financial, moral, spiritual, mental, psychological, even physical, and in every other way.

BUILDING CONVICTION QUALIFICATION

The *knowing* area is the second central component of growth and qualification as a missionary. We call it conviction.

Conviction is biblical and theological training and knowledge. It also involves comprehension and wise discernment, knowing how to put the pieces together. Often, a field missionary bumps into a theological conundrum. The new missionary may arrive at the wrong answers, or no answer, if they don't have the proper biblical understanding and framework to evaluate this theological conundrum. It would be a mistake to simply react or judge based on their own home-culture history. So, they need to be thoroughly trained in Bible knowledge. They need to have theological understanding of the basics of systematic theology and biblical theology. This biblical and theological training often occurs in a Bible school or seminary setting, or at least a formalized training setting. They need to understand church planting. They need to be a student of church planting and church leadership development.

The candidate needs to understand global missions and missions history, including the great biographies of missionaries. They need to understand global awareness, answering questions like: "What are current issues in missiology worldwide? What is the status of Christian missions in the region where we're going? What are the problems of the people of that region?"

The new missionary needs to understand timeless missiology. By timeless, we mean not just current fads and trends. What are the essentials proven over decades and generations that are biblical and strong? What do you need to get you to the intended result? What will, Lord willing, produce thriving indigenous local churches?

Lastly, conviction has an element of lifelong learning, aptitude, and commitment. A good missionary needs to have an attitude of being a lifelong learner. You always continue learning the language. You always continue learning the culture. You never stop learning how to grow in Christ and grow in grace so that you become more like Jesus. Lifelong learning is part of who we are and what we model. We continue to learn and grow personally to become more and more effective for the kingdom's sake.

BUILDING COMPETENCE QUALIFICATION

The third major area is competence, or *doing*. By that, we mean actual ministry skills experience. The candidate will learn through practical guidance, mentoring, and experience to gain the skills and competencies needed in their prospective ministry. They need firsthand experience.

The first bit is local-church-based experience. Are they experienced in local church ministries? Have they actually served in a variety of local church ministries? Do they get along with the people and the ministry teams they serve with?

The second element is life skills and experience. These are things that are outside the local church or maybe outside "spiritual" things. If they're going to a relatively closed country, they will need life skills to work in a business. Whether they work by contract or whether they create their own business, they need to have business skills. You can't send someone into another country, culture, and environment to start a business if you take someone straight out of college who's never worked a real job or been employed for very long beyond lawn mowing and babysitting. They need to understand accounting, marketing, customer relations skills, hiring and retaining staff, the supply chain, and those kinds of things. Do they have that kind of marketplace experience?

The third area of competence is missions strategy. Has the candidate wrestled with missions strategy, considering case studies and real-life examples similar to their projected ministry? Do they have experience working in or with a church planting team? Have they worked with overlapping authorities, each putting pressure on you differently? When you go overseas, you have to deal with all kinds of bureaucracy related to immigration and finances, issues related to the national church, the missions agency, the sending church, and your own family. No one ever has more bosses than a missionary in the field because they have all of these people who claim to have some slice of authority over their lives. They need practical strategic thinking about how all those things line up.

Next is short-term missions experience. Short-term missions experience is a great test and the beginning of learning to be a good missionary. Short-term missions experience opens their eyes to the realities of life in the field. With lengthening timeframes, they may progress from a one-week short-term missions experience to a term of two weeks, then to a month, six months, or even a year and a half or two years as an intern before they are commissioned as a missionary.

The next element of facilitation consists of advocacy and a Barnabas Team. This relates to the very first thing we said about mentoring. If the missionary candidate has someone from within the church who is walking alongside them as a mentor, an advocate, a friend, an encourager, a challenger, or a confronter, then that person becomes a part of what we call a Barnabas Team.

The new missionary needs ongoing advocacy within the church body—a smaller group that knows them more intimately and is able, willing, and committed to pray with and for them. The Barnabas Team works with them through finances, logistics, prayer, encouragement, schooling for their children, communication, and personal security. The advocacy team takes the lead in those areas on behalf of the whole church.

Competence also includes chemistry with people. Chemistry is a generic term for a consistent, godly way of working with people. Missionaries need to be people persons. A missionary task is a people-oriented task. If you're going to be a good missionary, you must learn how to get along with people and be outgoing enough to make friends with strangers and share the gospel with them. It seems obvious, but someone who is a recluse or a sharply defined introvert will have a tough time unless they change—and by God's grace, they can. We want to see chemistry with people, a people-oriented grace that enables the missionary to get along with others, make friends, expand their sphere of relationships, and influence others.

The last thing on competence is cross-cultural capacity. By this, we mean that the missionary candidate needs to have a growing intentionality in their understanding and appreciation for cross-cultural features, the culture itself, the practices, the holidays, and all those things. Just because someone likes to eat at Taco Bell doesn't mean they're a good cross-cultural missionary. We know of missionaries who thought they were perfectly qualified for the field, but when they got there, they couldn't stand eating rice daily. They ended up leaving the field because they didn't like the food. What kind of an excuse is that? Those competencies can be tested before a missionary goes to the field.

Missionaries can raise excuses about not understanding or liking the culture. However, it is essential to test cross-cultural capacity and aptitude in real-life experiences before they leave for the field. That's how to assess if they will be willing to stay for the long term for the sake of the ministry and the Lord.

We've run through this list of qualifications very quickly. The last question involves time: How long does it take? How long does it take for a missionary candidate to go from the beginning (saying, "I think God's calling me to be a missionary") to the end (the church commissioning them as a missionary)? It varies widely. In general, it will take at least a couple of years. In Paul's case, remember, it took twelve years from when he was called to when his sending church sent him out.

PATIENCE, PERSISTENCE, AND PURPOSE PAY OFF

It doesn't have to take twelve years! Different people enter the matrix of training and preparation with some skills already in their toolbox. Some people are already qualified in many ways before they begin the missionary journey. They may just need an update on their understanding of the culture, history, and current field issues before they leave. Some dear friends were early retirees when they started their journey to become missionaries. When asked about their field preparation, they told people, "God has prepared us for twenty-five years to leave to go to the field." We all can appreciate and respect that. They had been very intentional about living their life, so they were prepared to go to the field when the Lord called them.

If your missionary candidate has good marketplace experience, has matured as a Christian, has been effective in service in the church, and has been aggressive about learning all the things having to do with missions, their timeframe will be much shorter. Yet they still need to qualify in character, conviction, and competence as a leader in the church before they're sent out from the church to be missionaries. Those starting from the beginning, before graduating from high school, will take much longer. That time will give you much more input into their life to ensure they're ready when the church commissions them to go to the field. May God bless your efforts in restoring missions to the church by selecting, sending, and shepherding missionaries from your church.

COUNTDOWN TO LIFTOFF

Six months after arriving home from their exploratory trip, Kevin and Melissa, together with their Barnabas Team and the Missions Team, were planning a special weekend for their official commissioning as missionaries sent by Hopewell Bible Church. It seemed a long time since that first conversation with Pastor Aaron about wanting to become missionaries sent from HBC. In other ways, the time had flown by. The previous two-plus years were incredibly intense, deep, and rich. God changed their lives; they learned so much through preparing and becoming qualified as missionaries. Now they understood better how vital that training time was. Somewhere along the way, one of their elders, a retired military officer, said, "It's just like the military: plan to win, prepare to win, commit to win. Only in our case, it's winning people to the Lord and gathering them into their own churches to worship Him."

START THE ENGINES

The commissioning weekend arrived.

Friday night, there was a special thank-you dinner for the Hopewell elders, the Missions Team, and the Langfords' Barnabas Team. They sang, prayed, and heard some sweet stories about the process. There were many tears and hugs all around.

Saturday afternoon, there was a popcorn-and-cookies matinee viewing of a video created for them by techies in the church. It featured some brief interviews with Kevin and Melissa, Pastor Aaron, Missions Team elder Chuck Davis, and mentors Uncle Vernon and Sara Tennant, mixed in with a montage of their training experiences over the past thirty months. It was a fast-paced, heartfelt, and humorous history. The time closed with an open Q and A. The kids asked all the usual questions, like:

- How and when did you first feel called to become a missionary?
- What was the most challenging part of your preparation?
- What is the weirdest food you had "over there"?
- Can I have your cat when you leave?
- What scares you most about going?

The Langfords were up for it all.

Sunday morning was glorious! The Langfords gave a brief testimony and praised God for all He had done to enable them to go to their place in East Asia. The missions agency sent a representative to say how special it was to receive the Langfords into the field family and to see the extraordinary role of Hopewell Bible Church in the past, present, and future story. Pastor Aaron gave a special sermon from 3 John 5–8, teaching about the local church's role in sending and the blessing the church receives from that partnership. At the end, all the elders came around the Langfords on the stage to lay hands on them and pray for them as they were sent out.

The Langfords had a surprise announcement. No, it wasn't what everyone was thinking. It was an appeal for HBC to seek others to train and send to join them in the field! They wanted teammates from their sending church to join them.

Thankfully, the Barnabas Team had encouraged them to take five days between the commissioning service and departure flight. They could say goodbye to their families and close friends less hurriedly. They could rest a bit to recoup strength and stamina for what was facing them upon arrival in their new country. They could pack their baggage for departure with some sense of sanity rather than rushed panic.

LIFTOFF!

Twenty people from the church showed up at the airport to send off the Langfords. Of course, the group couldn't go beyond the check-in counter. But they huddled off to the side for another special dedicatory prayer and hugs all around. Teary-eyed and with hearts full of joy, Kevin and Melissa slipped into the queue for TSA security.

SEARCH FOR A STRATEGIC MISSIONS FOCUS

Securing the church's role in missions includes identifying a strategic direction for involvement. Having a strategic focus is new territory for most churches. In the past, churches have accepted the vision and focus of individual missionaries or their missions agency. Frequently, local churches have allowed others to provide them direction and initiative without input or question. Selecting a strategic focus is crucial for repatriating missions to the local church.

PROBLEMS OF NOT HAVING A STRATEGIC FOCUS

How can a local church become active, intentional, well informed, and prayerful in adopting a strategic focus for its missions outreach? Visiting a church and seeing a missions display with pins scattered all over the map is not a healthy indicator. If you ask what that church is doing in missions, their leaders likely will tell you they support some excellent things. However, there is usually no consistency in the types of ministry, intended results, people group targets, participation of the church in the ministry, and the amount of support funds given.

One of the root problems behind this scenario is that the church doesn't have an in-depth relationship with the missionaries and ministries they support. They can't have an in-depth relationship with someone or something they only support with $25, $50, or $100 monthly.

For example, a large church said their missions goal was to put a pin in every country on the world map in their lobby. They wanted to say they supported some "missions" ministry in every country. There are close to two hundred countries in the world! There is no way that their church family could have a personal relationship with and get involved in the ministry of that many missionaries. The type of ministry didn't seem to matter. Compatibility with the church didn't seem to matter. The goal of the ministry didn't matter. The only thing that mattered to this church was that it could put another pin in another country. Though this real example is extreme, it highlights why it is important to consider adopting a strategic focus.

DEFINING A STRATEGIC FOCUS

What is a strategic focus? A strategic focus in missions for a local church is the intentional selection of a specific geographic area, people group, project, or type of ministry that best expresses that church's part in completing the Great Commission. The people group concept has been beneficial in understanding how Christians may complete the Great Commission by seeing a vibrant, biblical church planted among every ethnicity on earth. Then, by default, a strategic focus often includes identifying a specific people group to reach with the gospel and church planting. The area or group selected might vary in demographic features, but it should be clearly identifiable as a distinct language group.

The choice of a strategic focus does not exclude everything else. Just because your church selects a particular type, location, ethnicity, or project does not mean you will stop being interested in other ministries. What it does mean is that your church will prioritize your strategic focus as you move forward in terms of attention, funding, relationship, and a sense of ownership.

BENEFITS OF A STRATEGIC FOCUS

Here are a few of the expected benefits of searching for and selecting a strategic missions focus:

1. The church will feel a higher sense of ownership regarding their missions outreach.

2. The church family can more easily grow to understand the culture, language, and challenges of that selected field.

3. Missionaries from your church have a ready-made pathway to a specific field ministry target, field team, and missions agency partner.

4. Because of the decluttering effect of a strategic focus, your church will have a more consistent stream of messaging and communication.

5. Relationships with the continuing missionaries will soar.

6. Choosing a strategic focus provides a rare opportunity to graciously trim missions commitments that don't fit with your more precise definition of missions or your strategic focus.

FOUNDATIONAL STEPS TOWARD IDENTIFYING A STRATEGIC FOCUS

We recommend taking some simple steps to help your church leadership make decisions on a strategic missions focus.

1. Clarify your church's biblical definition of missions to include the key elements covered in part 1 of this book. A good definition of missions includes understanding who sends, who qualifies as a missionary, and the sphere and goal of their work. Here is a short model definition of missions: "Missions is the sending out of specially equipped disciple-makers who cross barriers of distance, culture, and language to establish and strengthen the church in places beyond the normal sphere of influence of our members."

2. It is also valuable to stipulate the desired end goal or result of missions. Doing so resolves many concerns and potential conflicts about who and what kinds of ministries the church supports. As previously presented, ministry elements should aim toward that biblical end goal we call church planting. Missions in this view certainly includes ministries directly related to indigenous church planting, such as Bible translation, the training of indigenous church leaders, and ministries designed to enable the existing church to continue its church planting efforts. As per the Great Commission, activities include:

   - proclaiming the gospel
   - discipling believers and gathering them into a church
   - having biblically qualified shepherds who teach God's Word and oversee the administration of the ordinances

- meeting together weekly for worship, prayer, fellowship, and spiritual growth

NARROWING THE SCOPE OF WHO AND WHAT YOUR CHURCH SUPPORTS

We teach three different metrics to help determine who to support the most. The first metric identifies the level of relationship with your local church. This could partly be a matter of geographical proximity to your local church, but hopefully your church is raising candidates within it. The closer the candidate is to being a homegrown, ministry-active member of your church, the higher their score. They have a higher priority and get more support to go out from the church, representing the church in missions ministry.

The second metric has to do with priority or type of ministry. At the top of the line, we put church planting and development of indigenous local churches (that is, training indigenous leaders to continue church planting in their region or language group).

The third metric is access to the gospel. Here, the highest priority, with the highest metric value, would be unengaged, unreached people groups (UUPGs). These are places where there is no representative of Christianity. The next tier would be unreached people groups (UPGs) or unreached language groups. UPGs might have some Christian presence with only a weak church locally. They may be weak demographically, in influence, or in spiritual maturity. They need outside help to develop, grow, and multiply local churches within their ethnicity or language group.

SOME BIBLICAL SUPPORT FOR ADOPTING A STRATEGIC FOCUS

Combining those ideas lets you focus on where you want to go. It doesn't have to be something or someone you are already supporting. We'll get to the *how* element in just a moment, but let's start with the Scripture and see how Paul's mindset was to press to the edges of the gospel's reach continuously.

After being sent out from the church in Antioch, Paul went to Cyprus, Lycia, Pamphylia, Pisidia, Galatia, Asia, Mysia, Macedonia, Achaia, Italy, and then Spain. So, in provinces across the vast Roman Empire, Paul continued to press toward the edges of the gospel's reach. And that's what we ought to be thinking about today.

Here is Paul in Romans 15:18–24, which he wrote by the Holy Spirit:

> For I will not venture to speak of anything except what Christ has accomplished through me to bring the Gentiles to obedience—by word and deed, by the power of signs and wonders, by the power of the Spirit of God—so that from Jerusalem and all the way around to Illyricum I have fulfilled the ministry of the gospel of Christ; and thus I make it my ambition to preach the gospel, not where Christ has already been named, lest I build on someone else's foundation, but as it is written,
>
> > "Those who have never been told of him will see,
> > and those who have never heard will understand."
>
> This is the reason why I have so often been hindered from coming to you. But now, since I no longer have any room for work in these regions, and since I have longed for many

> years to come to you, I hope to see you in passing as I go to Spain, and to be helped on my journey there by you, once I have enjoyed your company for a while.

Paul made it clear that he kept pressing toward the edge. He systematically saw the gospel expand from Jerusalem all the way around to present-day Croatia, and he made it his ambition to preach the gospel, going not to those places where Christ had already been named, but to those places where the people hadn't heard and understood the gospel. For that reason, with strategic focus, he says, in effect, "Church in Rome, I expect to be helped on my journey to Spain by you." The word translated as "to be helped on my journey," as we have seen, is *propempo*.

Paul says the same thing slightly differently in 2 Corinthians 10:15-17:

> We do not boast beyond limit in the labors of others. But our hope is that as your faith increases, our area of influence among you may be greatly enlarged, so that we may preach the gospel in lands beyond you, without boasting of work already done in another's area of influence. "Let the one who boasts, boast in the Lord."

Paul even hints at this outward push in his letter to Titus, one of his last letters. Titus 3:12 reads, "When I send Artemas or Tychicus to you, do your best to come to me at Nicopolis, for I have decided to spend the winter there." He worked with Titus after he finished his ministry on the island of Crete to penetrate into Europe through the Balkan peninsula moving northward.

WHY SHOULD YOUR CHURCH SEARCH FOR AND SELECT A STRATEGIC FOCUS?

Let's answer a central question about this idea of a strategic focus: Why? We offer three reasons.

The first reason is for the church to clarify its focus on cross-cultural missions. The congregation needs to be able to wrap their minds around what they do in missions. The church should accept that it cannot do everything and thus should aim to do a few things well. The local church has to say "no" to many good things in order to have the freedom and resources to do the best things.

When your church has a strategic focus, your members understand that dynamic. Every church wants to proclaim, "We do missions well!" A strategic focus helps you actually do that. To be clear, it doesn't eliminate every other thing that you might support. You will always wrestle with legacy relationships or connections. However, your priority will be to accomplish the task of missions in a strategic area. Over time, that could shift as the task is completed in your original focus area. You might consider another location or language group or project. If your church has the capacity, you might be able to handle more than one strategic focus at a time. Likely, each one will be similar in need, ministry, and challenges.

As suggested earlier, a strategic focus does not have to be a specific geographical location or language group. A particular type of ministry may be your focus. One church surveyed their congregation and discovered that one-third of the adults were qualified and employed in medical professions. So, their strategic focus was opening new areas to the gospel through short-term medical clinics. It became an exciting journey for the whole congregation to participate in advancing the gospel with their specialty focus. We maintain that, whatever the type of ministry, it should be limited to directly contributing to raising indigenous local churches as the end goal.

The second reason to select a strategic focus is to simplify things. Too many choices paralyze us. We need to simplify our choices. This doesn't mean that all the other options are of less value to God, but they are of less value to the work that you have prayerfully discerned God has chosen for your church. When you make that choice, you lead your church to follow a particular direction for good reasons. God blesses a focused vision in more ways than may be evident initially. You can't do it all, but you can do your slice of the Great Commission excellently.

The third reason is that having a strategic focus amplifies involvement. More people can get involved when the goals and opportunities are clarified. They can wrap their hands around it. The goal is simplified. They don't have to do too many things. It's all focused on one thing. In so doing, you amplify the whole church's involvement through a strategic focus.

HOW DO WE SEARCH FOR AND SELECT A STRATEGIC FOCUS?

How do you arrive at a strategic focus? The first thing is to pray. You need to pray continuously that the Lord will guide you. Ask your church members to pray as you seek God's help to sharpen your church's missions focus. Even the missionaries and ministry you presently support should be informed: "Please pray with us because we are working toward adopting a strategic focus. We want to do what God wants us to do. Pray that we will make good decisions and have the right information."

Second, simply survey your opportunities. Begin by asking questions of those already in a relationship with the church.

Ask the missionaries and ministries you support:

- What places near to you are near to the edges of the gospel's reach?
- Where are you in relation to UPGs or indigenous churches needing leadership training for church planting?
- What do you think is the greatest need for seeing the gospel go to unreached or unengaged places around you?

Look at your church's relationships. Your church is probably in fellowship or association with local churches near you or in your like-minded circle. If you don't have someone to train and send from your congregation, maybe there is someone with whom you have an automatic relationship within your sphere of fellowship. There just might be a missionary you already know and trust that is going to a UPG. Is there someone you know who already represents one of those least reached places that your church can adopt as a strategic focus?

Third, survey your congregation. Who knows? You may have connections through business, ethnicity, or relationships that would guide you to a specific place that makes sense for your congregation. Ask about their heritage, the languages they speak, and their own personal history or knowledge of the unreached.

Fourth is a field study. By that, we mean gathering all the appropriate data. You can visit a number of websites that maintain demographic data, even maps and photos of the unreached of the world. Think through this demographic, statistical, and logistics data. Ease of transportation and communication across time zones may have a bearing. Churches east of the Mississippi may find it easier to think of going eastward to Europe, the Middle East, and Africa. Churches west of the Mississippi may find it easier to think of going westward to Asia. Still, think long-term about how easy or expensive it would be for your congregation to participate in the ministry.

The final step of the field study is taking a small entourage from the church to visit the field before making the final decision. Talk to missionaries with experience working in that area or a similar cultural setting. Visit missionaries in the field or fields in consideration. Ask a lot of questions. Try to picture what it would be like for your sent ones to live and work there. Ask questions like:

- What are the challenges and obstacles?
- How much will it cost?
- What are the security concerns?
- What are the political and immigration hurdles?
- What implications and particular stresses would life there have for our sent missionaries?
- Which missions agency is the best fit for our church and this work?
- Will that agency approve a mutual partnership agreement to facilitate our sending a missionary with them to that field?
- Are there specific teams to join and what details of their team ethos, structure, doctrine, methodology, and strategy should be considered?
- What special training and experience is needed for a worker sent out with this strategic focus?

WHAT IS THE ROLE OF THE MISSIONS AGENCY IN THE PROCESS?

The sending church's engagement and ownership in the process of seeking a strategic focus represents a paradigm shift in world missions. It requires adjustments on the part of both the local church and the missions agency. Missions-sending organizations undoubtedly play a significant role in helping a local church identify and follow through with a strategic focus. As the local church increases its missions engagement, the missions agency must likewise increase its skills and partnership in responding to the local church's involvement. At this point, we should consider what the missions agency can do to positively adapt to the church's initiative in selecting a strategic focus.

The track record of missions agencies is often unpleasant in this respect. Because missions agencies have grown to be protective of their turf, expertise, and imagined rights, they have tended to belittle the local church's authority and role in missions. Historically, missions organizations have grown to expect local churches to supply them with people (in recruits and volunteers), pesos, prayer, and platform time. Their missionaries can subtly reflect the same mindset, which says, in effect, "Church, you have no place here. You wouldn't understand. Let the agency do this for you."

A local church wanting more involvement in sending its people and choosing a field of focus will meet surprise and polite disparagement. Firsthand experience proves as much. The local church is not welcomed to the table as a partner, only as a benefactor. The agency doesn't ask, "How can we help you fulfill your dream?" Instead, they state, "Here are all the ways your church can help us fulfill our vision." "Partnership" agreements penned by the missions agency give a mere nod to the church's role while typically having the church and missionary sign away all their rights to the agency. We could go much further in documenting this attitude.

So, the first task is this: to respect the local church's rights, role, and intentions. Humbly and genuinely allow the church to assume their biblical role and responsibility for their ministry, missionary, and vision. Listen well. Allow the agency's resources to meet the specific world missions focus of the sending church. Seek how to enable the sending church partner to equip and validate their candidate's qualifications and shepherd their missionary. Facilitate the sending church's interaction with the agency (both at home and in the field) regarding goals, strategies, and methodologies matching their desired ends.

Not all sending churches will be asking for a partnership agreement. But the number that do so is growing. Not all churches will ask for help identifying a strategic focus. But it is an honor to be asked. Churches going through this process are the best kind of missions churches. As a missions agency, don't you want a steady stream of high-quality, long-term, well-supported, focused, and fruitful missionaries? Of course! Just allow for local church partnerships!

Second, missions agencies blessed to receive a request from this kind of church must learn how to work with churches to achieve their mutual goals. The agency must communicate to bridge the gap between the church and the fields of interest. Someone will likely have to visit the church, explain the agency's prefield requirements, and learn the church's overall plan for sending. The agency should be willing to facilitate an exploratory field visit to aid the church in selecting a strategic focus.

Third, the missions agency may need to appoint an individual to be the liaison with the church, monitoring and evaluating the resulting partnership agreement annually. Is it working? Where are the weak spots we could strengthen? Are there new issues that have popped up that we should address?

A partnership with a church will work out if the missions agency is open, humble, and respectful. After all, nearly every missions agency's founding documents claim that the agency is working on behalf of and serving the church. It is always challenging to do a new thing. There is no excuse for not doing the right thing.

RESULTS

Many churches have gone through the process of searching for and selecting a strategic focus. That process has challenged them to think deeply about their part in the Great Commission. This strategic thinking also translates into becoming more focused on a particular direction for local outreach. The church can say, "This is the local ministry we will emphasize and get our people involved in. It is where we send short-term ministry teams for exposure and experience before going across the ocean for cross-cultural ministry."

The church does not have to be large and affluent to get to this point. The church I served, with an average attendance of a little more than two hundred on Sunday mornings at that time, went through this prayerful, hopeful, faith-filled process. The elders approved a challenging strategic focus and drafted a visionary twenty-five-year plan for that missions focus. God has been pleased to bless the congregation's participation and ownership. The church has grown. The work overseas among unreached people has grown and developed. God gets the glory.

Occasionally, we have come into a larger church that can't decide on just one strategic focus. In one case, they created a threefold plan that would play out over ten years. For the first three years, they would be all-in on ministry in a limited-access country in East Asia. Then, while maintaining their relationship with that ministry, they would focus on a Muslim group for three years. Lastly, they would adopt a Buddhist UPG and thus have hit the largest segments of unreached people on the earth. In time, by God's grace, they did all of the above. They have a fantastic congregational ownership of those ministries. They communicated well and involved many congregation members in each strategic focus.

We strongly encourage you to prayerfully consider your church adopting a strategic focus in a way that is a game changer for helping your people understand, grasp, own, and take action on cutting-edge missions ministry to fulfill the Great Commission.

TEARY-EYED AND WITH HEARTS FULL OF JOY

Kevin and Melissa Langford arrived in the capital city of their newly adopted country after twenty-three hours in transit, including three flights spanning ten thousand miles. The host from their missions agency field team met them, along with their six suitcases. They felt emotionally and physically exhausted even though they had taken some time to rest before their departure day. Of course, they had experienced traveling on their earlier exploratory trip. But the weight of coming to stay felt very heavy on their hearts.

Thankfully, they knew what to expect:

- They began the staging process for long-term immigration visas.
- They had to survive the first week of sleepwalking to recover from jet lag.
- They lived in limited quarters as guests in someone else's house.
- They had no independent transportation.
- They had to get phones and transportable internet plans set up.
- They visited and enrolled in the language-learning program and set up tutors.
- They reintroduced their tummies to the national foods and spices.
- They remembered what it was like to live in a sheath of sweat.
- They began to recall the arduous registration process to create a business in their host country. They had decided on and prepared for what they planned to do. But the process was not something they looked forward to.

They were extremely grateful for WhatsApp, Skype, Zoom, email, and texting capabilities. They weren't just for communicating with their church, family, and friends. They were essential for connecting, coordinating with, and getting assistance from their teammates in the city. The Langfords, and whoever was on the other end of their communication, had to be careful to use the right words and terminology. Proper security protocols protected their long-term presence and that of their entire team in the field.

Kevin and Melissa ratcheted up their resolve to work hard on learning the national language. It was essential for their lives now. It would also give them a good foundation for learning the next language, that of their target unreached people group. Gone were the days when a missionary could just learn one foreign language for a lifetime of service. Some of their colleagues were working on their third or fourth language!

All the training and discipleship of the past two years came into play. Marriage relationship stress, straining to hear and duplicate strange language sounds, the relentless avalanche of new information and the expectation of being able to remember it all, physical and emotional adaptation, uncontrollable time pressures squeezing out personal spiritual reflection, the routine reminder that "they don't make coffee here like at home." It was all so exciting and draining at the same time! Their missions agency teammates were very helpful, if not always sympathetic with them, about the little things that bugged them.

Yet underneath it all, they had confidence that God had placed them there, just like they had dreamed. He would faithfully love them, show Himself gracious, and enable them to be good teammates for each other as a couple. They needed to take a deep breath and remind themselves of those truths daily. Kevin and Melissa didn't know how much they would come to need that confidence.

SPECIFY YOUR CHURCH'S MISSIONS RESOURCES

Strong missions churches, regardless of their size, are often seen as an incredible treasure trove for missionaries looking for support. A key secret skill of the leading pastor and the missions leader of the church is to be able to say "no" as the gatekeeper for the church. Missionaries of every kind want to present their ministry vision to the church.

The reason they must say "no" is so that they can say "yes" to the best things. Too easily dispersing and diffusing missions support contributes to ineffectiveness and lack of focus. It's not that the pastor or missions leadership can't be interested in the work of solid missionaries wherever they exist in the world. It's that church leaders shouldn't allow just anyone to win the hearts and minds of their church people, especially when those seeking support do not align with the church's chosen values, priorities, and focus.

GUIDING DEFINITIONS AND VALUES

Thus, we must address guidance for priorities in missions funding. Many churches have applied the information we will describe here to determine precisely how and how much they will support missionaries, whether they come from their own church or other sending churches.

If the church articulates its values well, everyone will be clear on what ministries might be acceptable and which would be out of bounds. We coach and consult with churches to express the framework of acceptability in writing.

- Start with a sound biblical definition of missions.
- Build a clear definition of a missionary. Here are common elements we have articulated earlier:
  » specially trained and biblically qualified
  » engaged in cross-cultural ministry
  » aimed at church planting or church leadership development in a strategic area or people group
  » affirmed by and sent from the local church
- Missionaries must substantially agree with the church's doctrine and distinctives.
- Priority in relationships and funding goes to missionaries who have been active church members.
- Support fewer missionaries but at higher support levels in order to be more focused and to develop deeper church involvement, ownership, and relationships.

AN INTERVIEW OR APPLICATION PROCESS

How do you find out this kind of information from a potential supported missionary? The starting point is simply to ask them. Find out if they align with your church and your church's guiding values in missions. You can begin to know a candidate for support with a clear and comprehensive application that answers the following questions:

- Who are they (schooling, marriage, family, alliances, testimony)?

- What is their specific training and experience, and how has their sending church validated their calling?

- Who is their sending church, and where is "home" to them? (It rarely makes sense to support someone based a long distance from your church if you want to build a close relationship with them for the long term.)

- What is their missions ministry or proposed ministry? What is the planned goal and strategy or methodology they will pursue?

- What is their missions agency, and how did they choose it?

Overall, the application should allow the candidate to get at least some sense of their character, conviction, and competencies on paper.

THREE KEY METRICS TO PRIORITIZE SUPPORT

Here is a simple conceptual mechanism for helping you prioritize missions support, which we introduced in the previous chapter. When teaching this in person, we often refer to this as the "*X, Y, Z,*" or the three axes of support. But for the sake of simplicity here, let's think in terms of three columns.

The three columns describe three critical components of priority for supporting missions. The columns represent the three priorities of the church for support:

- First column: relationship to the church
- Second column: ministry priorities
- Third column: access to the gospel

The top of each column is the highest level one could achieve in evaluating their potential financial support level. The top is the highest rank or priority. The five cells of each column are ranked one through five, with five at the top. The missionary candidate for support is assessed in each priority column. Their score or descriptor level helps the Missions Team determine where this candidate falls in the spectrum of possible funding. Some churches have placed dollar numbers associated with each cell ranking. As you move up or down the ranking of each column, predefined amounts of funding may be related to those descriptors. The missionary qualifying to get the most funding would be someone who scores the highest in each column: relationship to the church, ministry priorities, and access to the gospel. We will describe a hypothetical case below.

THE FIRST COLUMN RANKING IS FOR THE RELATIONSHIP TO THE CHURCH

Each column has "5" as the highest score at the top and goes down to "1" as the lowest score at the bottom.

5. The top cell is for someone raised in the church. This candidate has been mentored and trained in your church setting. You've tracked and helped equip them from their first inklings of missionary interest.

4. The next cell down is for a church member who has been active in church life and serving in church ministries for at least four or five years.

3. The middle cell of this priority column is for a newer church member who is growing in relationships and serving in church ministries. It could be someone who is a 5 (top-level candidate) in relation to a nearby sister or like-minded church.

2. This cell is for someone newly accepted into church membership or new to a like-minded church near your church. They are not seasoned in your church culture and may need a lot of orientation to the foundations of your church's doctrine and culture, especially in the area of missions.

1. This candidate has no relationship with your church at all. They might not have a historical base in your area or even be known to your affiliated church relationships. Typically, you would not consider supporting this candidate.

THE SECOND COLUMN RANKING IS FOR MINISTRY PRIORITIES

5. The highest ministry priority is pioneering church planting and leadership development for training indigenous church planters. Things decisively connected to that kind of church

planting could be included here (e.g., Bible translation as a component of church planting).

4. The next priority would be ministries that directly support church planting and training of church planters. This level could include ministries such as field leadership and consulting with church planting teams. Some ministries may equip indigenous pastors to develop businesses to support themselves for church planting. They might provide or support a liaison for literacy to teach people how to read the Bible in their own language. Creative evangelism and discipleship directly related to growing young church plants might qualify here.

3. The middle priority in this column would be ministries that support church planting, leader training, and multiplication efforts. Ministries aimed to strengthen and extend the reach of indigenous churches might include publication and various means of communication, including social media, electronic, and internet evangelism, teaching, and discipleship.

2. Cell number two in this column would be service and support ministries and methodologies that don't have a clear connection to the church planting regime but are still supportive of that end goal. This class could include community development, self-sufficiency training (especially for new Christians ostracized by the dominant culture), and specialty ministries like youth, music, sports, affinity interest groups, etc.

1. Last in this column are ministries that don't match up with the above priorities. Sometimes, missionaries have not consciously considered how their specialty ministry either complements or competes with the highest priority of church planting and church leadership development. A challenge to them could provide guidance and benefit to their ministry philosophy and plans. Typically, you would not consider supporting this candidate.

THE THIRD COLUMN RANKING IS ACCESS TO THE GOSPEL

5. This descriptor is easy: the candidate targeting an unengaged, unreached people group (UUPG) is of the highest priority. A UUPG has no known Christian witness residing among them.

4. The candidate planning to enter an unreached people group (UPG) is next in priority for access to the gospel. Demographically, evangelicals make up less than 5 percent of the population of a UPG group. Statistically, it is difficult for those Christians to plant churches and grow to evangelize their people without help from outside.

3. The middle priority descriptor is for a new initiative for pioneering church planting in a place or people group target. It may be in a de-Christianized or Western country that has had a radical decline in the presence of biblical Christian influence. It has little to no available Christian witness and is in need of gospel-teaching churches. What

churches exist may be weak and in need of sustained Bible teaching.

2. This cell in the priority list would be supportive ministries that supplement or assist entry to the higher-level priorities. These ministries might be more institutional or technical. They often arise out of long-term missions ministries to sustain growth in the indigenous church but are not themselves planting churches or training leaders.

1. The last priority in the list would be a type of ministry not intentionally related to the indigenous church at all. It could involve administrative support for missionary work through building, management, immigration services, etc. It could involve ancillary work in the arts or secular education. Typically, you would not consider supporting this candidate.

Hypothetically, in this priority structure, you assign a dollar amount to each cell and add the numbers to determine the support level. For example, if each of the cells numbered 2 through 5 added $250 per month of support per step, then each column could have a maximum of $1,000. The highest resulting sum committed would be $3,000 per month for a missionary trained and sent by your church to do church planting in a UUPG. Your church would decline to give regular financial support to a candidate scoring a level 1 on any of the three priority columns.

The scenario above is hypothetical. Your church's missions-support capabilities and inclinations might lead you to redefine the columns and the financial scale accordingly. Good, godly leaders in the church might agree to elements quite different than our example. Still, the point is that establishing clear definitions and metrics that are important to your church and your consideration of a missionary for support is invaluable. Doing so eliminates repetitive haggling and lengthy discussions about principles. Adopting a schema like this does not mean there can't be exceptions or revisions to the matrix of definitions used. What it means is that you have consensus and an established guide that gives you confidence and freedom to do the right thing.

PROBLEMS WITH SHIFTING DEFINITIONS

It may be helpful to address one complicated scenario we see too often in the field. It is the dilemma of shifting definitions. We've seen and heard of well-meaning missionaries who go to a challenging field and plant a church only to stay as the head pastor of that church for the rest of their life. In one sense, that might be called church planting. However, suppose some years after the launch of that single church, the expatriate missionary is still the sole pastor/elder in the church there. There is not an indigenous pastor installed or an indigenous plurality of elders responsible for the ministry in that church. In that case, it is no longer a church plant. That missionary is no longer a missionary but a pastor in a foreign country. It should be up to his sending church and supporting churches to help him understand the difference, including the consequence of withdrawing support. That "church plant" is unhealthy in several ways. It cannot be called an indigenous church by the historical definition of an indigenous church. It is not self-supported, self-governing, and self-propagating. The supporting and sending churches need to have an accountable relationship with the missionary such that this shifting definition of "church plant" never occurs.

APPLYING THE SUPPORT SPECIFICATIONS

The ranking system outlined above surely does not cover every possible scenario when it comes to determining church missions support. However, because it provides an organized and thoughtful way of approaching the support issue, it has proven effective for most churches to adopt this prioritization concept. It shortens the decision cycle and gives clarity to everyone affected. If you were to use this metric to review the missionaries you presently support, you could easily see where they fit in terms of priorities.

An interesting little dynamic is that when missionary candidates become aware of this prioritization on the part of the sending church, they aim for the top levels. Which is precisely what you want them to do. They will aim to have the best insider relationship with the local church, double down on indigenous church planting, and seek to target their ministry to those with the least access to the gospel. That's what we all want, by God's grace.

HITTING A WALL

Six months in, the Langfords hit a wall. They didn't think it would happen to them. They had prepared so well. Yet their training had informed them that, likely, it would happen to them.

They were adjusting well. They had shown so much discipline and attention to language learning. They imbibed all they could from the more experienced missionaries in their circle of relationships. But one morning, they woke up with their hopeful optimism unexpectedly deflated. The excitement of the newness of things and the wide-eyed tourist attitude had worn off. Somehow, it hit them that all this hard work was just scratching the surface of all the hard work yet to come. So many unanswered questions about the future circulated through their minds: Would they ever get this language? Would they ever figure out the grammar? Would they ever be able to pronounce things even close to how a native speaker spoke, close enough to be understood? More than just speaking, when would they be able to read and write even as well as an elementary school kid? When would they get the vocabulary to express the normal things of life, much less the intangible truths of the gospel?

It wasn't just the steep climb of language and culture ahead that discouraged them. It seemed to be life in general. They missed home so much. They missed their friends at Hopewell Bible Church. Everyone and everything was different here. Weekly WhatsApp or Skype video check-in calls just weren't enough. Kevin and Melissa cried together. Then they prayed to God to send a ray of sunshine to their oppressively gloomy hearts. It seemed like such a defeat to even feel this way!

Much to their relief, help was on the way. Hopewell's leaders and the Barnabas Team also had learned in training that the Langfords might hit a wall at six months. Unbeknownst to Kevin and Melissa, Uncle Vernon and Sara Tennant, the Langfords' dear mentor friends, had planned all along to visit them in the field at their seven-month mark. With the approval and resourcing of the HBC leaders and the Langfords' Barnabas Team, the Tennants made the long trip to visit, encourage, and counsel their beloved mentees in the field.

The Tennants' field visit was a whirlwind nine days. There were introductions to the Langfords' leaders, neighbors, language school staff, and friends. Kevin and Melissa acted as guides for a quick tour of their city. Then the Tennants had arranged with the Langfords' team leader for the four of them to get away to a retreat in the same geographical vicinity as their intended unreached people group. Kevin and Melissa had to stretch their limited language skills with hand motions. They spent most of their time talking, praying, counseling, and taking long walks. It was a glorious time of recharging and recommitting. During that retreat, away from the language school setting, Kevin and Melissa were far from discouraged. They were actually surprised at how the immersion setting forced their comprehension and expression of the language to emerge.

Of course, the Langfords had a long way to go to the finish line of this first marathon, which consisted of language proficiency, cultural acquisition, long-term visa acquisition, and fine-tuning their strategy for entry and relocation to ministry in their UPG area. Even before they cried out to Him, God heard and answered their prayers for help. The Tennants' loving care and ministry infused Kevin and Melissa with new energy and resolve to press on.

STIMULATE YOUR CONGREGATION FOR MISSIONS INVOLVEMENT

The principal shift needed by the typical church missions ministry is to change the role of the church leaders and the Missions Team (or Missions Committee). Traditionally, church leaders think of themselves and the Missions Team as having the authority to do everything in the realm of world missions on behalf of the congregation. Here, we recommend that leaders prioritize mobilizing the congregation for missions involvement.

Let's consider what this shift means and how it plays out practically in a local church. Routine administrative items on the agenda will still get delegated to the church leaders and Missions Team. There will be issues and events that they must decide on, plan, and organize. Still, one of the primary purposes of their charter should be to build a family ethos in which every member has an active role in missions.

EVERY MEMBER HAS A PART TO PLAY

A straightforward concept that supports this goal is to think of every congregant as a world Christian. What is a "world Christian"? A world Christian aligns their life to benefit the gospel and the Great Commission. Doing so means they realize they have a part in the Great Commission. At a minimum, every Christian can pray for missionaries and the completion of the Great Commission. Everyone can be the sender at some level.

Every Christian can give something of their treasure, time, or talent in stewardship for the sake of missions. They have a role in stewardship even if they're not the sent one, the "go-er." Every Christian has a role in the local sense of being evangelistically active. They can live their life for the gospel in such a way that people around them know that they're Christians. Every church member can grow to actively seize opportunities to have gospel conversations, host gospel Bible studies, and invite people to gospel events. As they live out their lives in light of the Great Commission, they are world Christians. The result of having a missions-mobilized congregation is that every member is aware of and taking action to be a missions-minded Christian. They know their roles. They step up to do them.

JERUSALEM TO THE END OF THE EARTH IS SIMULTANEOUS

The church leadership and Missions Team don't allow the church to conclude that Acts 1:8 is sequential, thinking, "Let me just focus on my Jerusalem. Let others think about reaching the ends of the earth." As we have seen, the grammar is simultaneous and inclusive. Acts 1:8 shows the concentric rings of influence as "both-and" conjunctions. It doesn't teach that all Christians should distribute themselves equidistantly from each other around the land area of the globe. However, it implies that the church needs to consider building a strategy for priorities in each sphere: Jerusalem, Judea, Samaria, and the ends of the earth ("all nations" per Matthew 28:19).

CREATE OPPORTUNITIES FOR INVOLVEMENT

The Missions Team educates, inspires, and creates opportunities for the congregation to fulfill their biblical role as a church. It inspires action at the grassroots. People in the congregation are trained and encouraged to develop cross-cultural relationships with people locally. They should be prompted to participate in missionary support, encouragement, and visitation. Congregants can organize and participate in short-term missions trips to do specific things in the ministry of their missionaries.

THE CHURCH HAS A MISSIONARY-TRAINING PROTOCOL

Whole-church mobilization also means that the church has a training pipeline through which church members are equipped and sent to be missionaries to fulfill the strategic focus of the church. Church leaders don't allow church members to build expectations that the church supports just any ministry out there. There is an equipping, nurturing, and focusing ministry on the part of the church to ensure that it sends people out who align with them in every way.

There are other ways in which the Missions Team can focus energies and initiatives locally to align with the church's goals and relationships. It's rare for a church to be outside the reach of a metropolitan area where there is a significant ethnic or immigrant community to which they can minister in some way for the sake of the gospel. Accessibility becomes an opportunity to grow in cross-cultural exposure and skills. The church family learns in this context and uses it as a stepping stone for global missions and missionary training. That would be a "Samaria" type of place.

Mobilizing the whole congregation in missions means that the church leadership, the elders, and the Missions Team understand and take responsibility for training and equipping missionaries from their congregation. The church should not automatically assume that the missionary-training institution (like a Bible school or seminary) or the missions-sending agency prepares the candidate comprehensively enough to fulfill all qualifications needed for long-term ministry in a cross-cultural missions field. The church will need wise counsel and help to get started in prefield missionary training. However, it is possible and important for the church to take the challenge. To the point of this chapter, missionary training will require a lot of congregational involvement in the process.

We want to see that the church is involved with a goal and vision of raising new missionaries from their congregation, whether small or large. One could argue that a large church has more potential in this respect. Per capita, however, medium and smaller churches do more of the hands-on, nitty-gritty work of stewardship and missionary production. Years ago, a missions field leader said he would prefer a missionary raised in a rural farm area to a missionary raised in a metropolitan area from a wealthy megachurch. The reason is quite realistic. Guys from farm country, in general, are creative and not afraid to attempt something that they haven't done previously. They know how to use whatever tools and materials are available. They're comparatively self-sufficient. Candidates raised in an urban or suburban setting, especially in a large church, often have a lot of assumptions. They may never have needed to be creative. They expect many things to be provided for them the way they were in their more affluent church context. They miss the convenience and availability of everything they like. You know you're in trouble when someone arriving in a missions field for the first time immediately checks their phone to find the nearest Starbucks.

In all seriousness, we would take either candidate—the farm country guy or the city guy from a large church. However, we would work closely with them and their sending church to ensure they are trained well. Nothing has more potential to ignite and sharpen the missions vision of a church than getting skin in the game by sending candidates raised in that church. These beloved candidates have deep relationships with your church family. They will very much be representatives of your church, sent out to do what your church cannot otherwise do and, eventually, by God's grace, to see churches planted where there are few or no churches.

ALL OF CHURCH LIFE CAN BE INFUSED WITH MISSIONS

Mobilizing your whole church means you begin to infuse missions teaching drawn from the Bible and illustrated through biographies, practical examples, and exposure to missionaries into all of your church's age groups and ministries. Teach your musicians some great missions or bilingual Christian songs to lead the congregation in singing. Teach your children to know and appreciate things about the world and the privilege of knowing the gospel, sharing it with their friends, and seeing people, even children from other cultures, come in contact with it. Promote and use great missionary biographies to challenge people's spiritual growth and connection to world missions. Expose them through short-term missions trips (STMs) designed to give them an appreciation for real missions life. Design trips with a spiritual component, not just to paint a building or to put a roof over a tribal church meeting place. Plan so that every STM participant interacts with and grows in respect and love for the missionary who sacrificed to live there.

For some people, the missions exposure may mean they feel a particular compulsion from the Lord to move in the direction of missions. If so, pour fuel on the fire. This mindset may help your congregation more warmly receive ethnic visitors into your congregation. Whether from Asia, Latin America, or Africa, your visitors may be ethnic people in your community. Be full of gospel grace and warmth, welcome them, and train your congregation to do so as well. Church members will have their eyes opened to more ways to be used for the Lord and the gospel, both locally and across the seas.

Another practical aspect is prayer. If you are injecting opportunities for people to pray for missions and missionaries in specific ways, it starts to get more real to them. It's in their heart. It's on their lips. They're looking for where the answers are to those prayers. To fuel those prayers, of course, you need to have regular and somewhat frequent communication with the missionaries that you support. They can let you know what are the newest requests or challenges and what are the blessings and answers to prayer that God is giving them because of your congregation's involvement. Have your small groups, Sunday school classes, and children's ministry adopt a missionary ministry to pray for regularly. Develop communication through your website or make it available in print for monthly prayer updates. Make sure to feature Sunday morning prayer for missionaries in a regular cycle.

SHORT-TERM MISSIONS TRIPS (STMS)

STMs can become a problem without a framework of convictions to guide and direct the pressures to do things. It takes immense energy and staffing to execute an STM on an annual basis. Without a clear connection to the gospel and a local church, trips or projects are indistinguishable from secular development or relief.

Design the STM to be a win-win-win for all involved—that is, a win for the missionary hosts in the field, a win for the STM participants in terms of spiritual growth and having a positive cross-cultural ministry experience, and a win for the target population in terms of exposure to the gospel and having a positive spiritual impact.

We recommend building an STM framework that works like a spiral curriculum. Each stage of the curriculum aims for more maturity, time, distance, and missions commitment. STMs are incredible tools for spiritual discipleship and formation for all involved, particularly for the potential missionary candidate. It's remarkable how much training and preparation an STM participant will accept to qualify for the trip. Keeping good personnel records will help you identify those who are committed and gifted for future missionary ministry.

DESIGNING A SPIRAL CURRICULUM FOR STMS

A spiral curriculum might consist of the levels listed below:

1. Middle schoolers can be taught about a biblical servant mindset, obedience to authority, and the personal spiritual benefits of a local STM, which assists a local ministry that needs labor-intensive help. The experience can be planned to take one week, during the weekdays. The team participants

can be trained for a couple of Saturday mornings before the week of service.

2. High school students can go cross-cultural without having to travel far. For some churches, this might be an ethnic community within one day of travel. Examples include Appalachian, First Nation/Native American, or immigrant communities, or even nearby international settings. The high schoolers are taught about that community's culture and history, as well as the development of biblical Christianity within it. They are trained in the basic greetings and phrases of their target STM language. They also train in their roles for spiritual ministries, such as putting on a Vacation Bible School or TESL (Teaching English as a Second Language) camp, or conducting evangelism events or literature distributions. All this should be connected to a local sponsoring church, church plant, or supported missions ministry. High schoolers can receive training and do fundraising for the STM over several months, culminating in the actual trip of seven to fourteen days. After the trip, it is important to conserve the spiritual fruit of the STM by meeting with the team or group to debrief on all aspects of the STM, especially its spiritual impact. A public report on the STM is a given.

3. College-aged young people who have participated in earlier parts of the spiral STM curriculum might be involved in a smaller team with a longer duration in an international context. Depending on the target ministry's relationship with the church, this could entail anything from being a

part of a specific outreach program for the better part of the summer, being a nanny for a supported missionary in need of one for several months to a year, participating in an internship and exposure trip with other young adults to a particular field for two to six weeks to test their calling, or receiving orientation to missionary life and work through a defined project or exposure agenda. The point is that this level requires a higher commitment of time, effort, funding, distance, and missionary intensity. Coming home, this young adult would also have an intensive debrief about the spiritual impact on their life and the STM's longer-term import for their desire to be vocationally involved in missions.

4. Post-college adults who have proven their abilities and are open to career service may enter a stage where the details are even longer-term but more specifically aimed at prefield missionary training. This type of STM normally occurs in the context of an ongoing conversation with church leaders about missions intentions and vision. The situation would probably be connected to the church's strategic focus. Opportunities could be created for this person, couple, or family to serve in a missionary internship or as a trainee. This term would be three to twelve months and require study, reflection, reporting, and accountability.

5. Families might go on their own STMs. A special opportunity could be created to provide an environment for one or more families to visit a missionary family with children of similar age. The purpose of the trip would be to encourage the host

family in the field and to ignite a love for missions among the visiting family members. The church could provide orientation, logistical support, and prefield training to the families involved. The families involved could manage the administration of this kind of trip themselves.

"Missions junkies" may present a special concern. They are the ones who want to go on every STM trip—the more distant, rugged, and exotic, the better. They have more selfie photos than any other kind. They are totally unhindered by fundraising for their trips. They may claim that they want to become full-time missionaries. They may even have gifts in language acquisition or cross-cultural skills. Yet they never want to work hard at study and in local church ministries to become qualified. Here's how to handle missions junkies: Bring them onto your STM planning, training, and leadership team. Expose them to, and insist that they embrace, a vision for using their passion for missions to help the church have an effective and meaningful STM ministry. If they are not willing to use their special love for STMs to serve the church and serve other participants, then they can't keep going on STMs. Further, the church won't sponsor or otherwise enable the recalcitrant missions junkie to go on STMs organized by other groups outside the church.

In line with the concept of mobilizing the whole church in missions, your church should have an annual event to highlight missions biblically and practically. A missions conference weekend will dedicate more specific prayer time to missions and encourage missions awareness and involvement in many ways.

You can also influence a world Christian pattern in families' home devotions. Recommend great books and resources for them. There are websites, printed materials, digital materials, and videos that you can use to stimulate more missions awareness and involvement.

By God's grace, as the whole congregation is mobilized in missions involvement, you will see a new generation of missionaries raised up and sent well from local churches to all nations.

RESOLVE TO PRESS ON

Kevin and Melissa learned the hard-won disciplines of contentment, trusting the providence of a loving Savior, and giving up their American assumptions about "personal rights." They have passed the two-year mark since immigrating to build a new home and ministry in their adopted country.

After taking the interactive oral and written FSI exams (tests administered by the U.S. Foreign Service Institute) in the national language, they were delighted that they both tested at Level 3+ out of 5 in language proficiency. They were free to relocate to their unreached people group and begin learning that language for their long-term ministry.

They made several informal "get acquainted" visits and two more information-gathering trips to the target area. They already made a few friends in their people group. Their field leadership and HBC gave them the green light to move. By God's grace, one of those early friends in a strategically located town had connections to a local house available for rent that was close to the market and not too far from access to fellow workers in an adjacent ministry group.

Kevin asked many questions to prepare himself for refurbishing the local house to make it more livable. Though excited, he and Melissa were concerned about starting language learning without having a preassigned tutor, meaning they would work out that process largely on their own. There would be so many things to learn about the culture of "their" people: new foods, new social cues, new friends to make, and new rhythms of life.

With a mixture of joy, faith, and trepidation, they made the move.

SUSTAIN A MISSIONS CULTURE IN YOUR CHURCH

How does every ministry in the church express its connection to the global overarching purpose of God to reach all nations with the gospel of Christ for His glory?

First of all, through prayer. Prayer is essential. God uses prayer as His instrument to accomplish His will on earth. Prayer should be natural to every Christian. In public prayer, prayer for missions and purposes should be woven into the church's warp, woof, and lifeblood. To facilitate prayer in family and private life, the Missions Team can create some practical tools. Simple help, whether in print or online, can inform and enable church members to pray with current information about the needs at hand.

MISSIONS FUEL FOR FAMILY DEVOTIONS

Family devotions are the second key to sustaining the church's missions culture. It's a wonderful help to make available missions-related materials for family devotions. In our family's life, we've enjoyed looking at missionary biographies or stories of children from other cultures to which missionaries are sent to teach the gospel and plant churches. Newsletters from your church's missionaries can be used in family devotions as a stepping stone to guide your thoughts and prayers about specific missions prayer requests.

MISSIONS CLASSES

The third key is ensuring the biblical and theological foundations of missions. At least every two to three years, offer an elective "Introduction to Missions" or "Missions 101" class for young people and adults. You will want to refresh everyone's minds about the local church's role in missions and how that works out in your church. Make it possible for youth and adults alike to learn biblical and theological insights on missions through the church's regular Bible teaching. Other interesting and typical topics for classes or small groups might include series on missions history or famous missionaries that you ought to know, the global status of missions, current trends in missions, missions strategy and church planting, the missionary-training process, missionary care, missionary candidate mentoring, and the schooling of missionary kids in the field.

CLASS OR SMALL GROUP MISSIONS ADVOCATES

Continue to feed an interest in missions throughout classes and small groups. Ensure that every class knows and "owns" a specific missionary family or missions ministry. Every class or small group can have a missionary family from whom they routinely receive information, status updates, and prayer requests. Providing that stream of information can partly be the responsibility of the Barnabas Team for your church's sent ones. If every class or small group owns a particular missionary family, one person in the class might be appointed to be a missionary advocate for that particular missionary. That advocate then becomes the point of contact for their class or small group updates.

SPECIAL SUPPORT FOR THE MISSIONARY COMING HOME

The Barnabas Team's role really increases in activity and importance when their missionary comes back for a Home Assignment or to return permanently. When your missionary visits your church (or resides on Home Assignment), the missions advocates get together to care for them. Housing, transportation, health needs, internet access, mobile phones, shopping needs, medical needs—whatever their needs are, the church is alerted to try to fulfill those needs while they're with you.

MUSIC

Every musical group or worship team should do a foreign language song at some point in the year, especially around whatever missions emphasis time is on your church calendar. Featuring Christians from other parts of the world using their ethnic music and instruments as a special feature during a worship service is a good opportunity to get people attuned to thinking about other cultures and how the gospel impacts people from other nations.

CULTURAL AWARENESS IN YOUR COMMUNITY

When your church is developing a missions culture, it's not unusual for people in the congregation to have their antennae up to notice people who dress differently than them or speak with a different accent than they're used to. They go to those people and ask, "Where are you from? Where did your family come from? How long have you lived here? Welcome to America!" They begin to open up their hearts and reinforce a missions culture as they recognize and are sensitive to the spiritual needs of people who are different from themselves.

SPONTANEOUS MISSIONS INITIATIVE

How can you tell that your missions culture is effective? One little test might help you answer that question. Your missions culture is effective when your congregation takes initiative. You notice your church members taking their own actions to share the gospel with someone different from them. You hear a report of a member crossing the lines of geography, language, or culture in order to proclaim and demonstrate Christ. You observe a church group, without having a direct plan or acting through a program of the church, start a ministry to needy people in your community for the sake of the gospel. Then you know that your church has a missions culture. May it be so in all of our churches.

MOVE MADE

Kevin and Melissa were starting over again. They had a new home. It was almost like déjà vu from their first arrival in the field. To be sure, the culture and language were not so foreign to them this time. Many features were similar. Still, they had to figure out new foods, neighbors, friendships in the community, the local authorities, and marketing patterns. They acquired a 125cc motorcycle with a sidecar in order to have independent transportation. They had the comforting assurance that their church was praying for them in the transition.

Back home at Hopewell Bible Church, the Missions Team led the church in their second annual missions conference. The Lord had graciously given HBC a long stretch of good missions development. More and more of the church body was directly involved in missions. Local opportunities for gospel outreach and cross-cultural connections seemed to spring up from the interests and initiatives of church members. HBC's UPG focus was a magnet for others with similar interests.

One of the features of the missions conference was a video report from the Langfords. The whole church was spellbound by the visual review of God's great work in the Langfords' ministry. The church's love made them feel like they were present in the scenes on the screen. Kevin and Melissa expressed their deep gratitude for the church's partnership. They also reminded HBC of their appeal to send coworkers to join their ministry team. "By God's grace, we know we couldn't be here without your prayers and support," they said.

Applause and tears of joy followed. So did prayer. The church was thankful to be "holding the ropes."

SEND AND SHEPHERD YOUR MISSIONARY WELL

Churches send up a distress signal to us when their missionary is in trouble. We now expect to receive a call or urgent email every month asking for counsel and help in such situations. Typically, the crisis is recent news to the church about their missionary, whether it is related to marriage and family, field relationships, or political concerns in the host country.

In one case, the pastor reported that their church elders had invested approximately one hundred hours of counsel and care for a challenging missionary situation in the field. In hindsight, we agreed that if the church had asked more probing questions of the missionary couple before they went to the field, the church might have reduced that time by 80 or 90 percent. Further, the issue might have been mitigated before it rose to a crisis level. An ounce of prevention is worth a pound of cure.

Sending and shepherding your missionary well will benefit your missionary, church, and field ministry enormously. Doing so is also essential to preventing your missionary from being so discouraged and disappointed that he resigns from the ministry. The role of the local church in sending and shepherding is an irreplaceable factor in avoiding the preventable loss of long-term missionaries to field ministry. So, we will take a closer look at attrition and its causes. The point of this chapter is to prepare the church body for sending and shepherding well.

ARMOR AGAINST ATTRITION

Attrition in the missions context refers to the reduction or loss of missionary staff by departure from the field. Planned attrition might result from retirement, or from the nationalization or downsizing of an area of ministry. Unplanned attrition can result from unpreventable factors like civil wars, evacuations, local government pressures, natural disasters, medical emergencies, or sudden family responsibilities. Unplanned but preventable attrition comes when missionaries resign and leave the field early for reasons they had not anticipated or prepared for. Reasons cited for preventable attrition often include incompatibility with fellow workers or the missions agency's administration, failure to adapt to the culture, a living environment that is unacceptable to the missionary, disillusionment, and an inability to cope with the demands of missions work.

Cross-cultural ministry is hard, particularly among the world's unreached people groups. This part of the world is becoming increasingly more hostile to missionary workers. It's not surprising that a lot of people drop out. There is a disparity among multiple sources in defining the metrics of attrition. But it's fair to say, in round numbers, that approximately 6,500 career missionaries leave the field each year, not planning on returning.

Some attrition is truly unpreventable. Having the best missions agency and the most engaged, resourceful sending church doesn't prevent all attrition. Plenty of real-life matters beyond the control of missions agencies and missionaries can force missionaries to return to their home countries. Of course, the good sending church then becomes deeply involved with restorative counsel, reentry, redirection, and resettlement into life at "home."

THE GRAVITY OF PREVENTABLE ATTRITION PROBLEMS

Around 71 percent of new missionaries arriving in the field resign within ten years due to preventable reasons. It costs a lot of money to send a missionary to the field. It might cost $300,000 to get a couple through their training and support-raising and then cover the launching funds they need to settle in a foreign country, including a year or more of language training. Almost half of those missionaries leave within the first five years, and that rate rises to 75 percent in the more challenging fields of service. For comparison, career missionary attrition rates in the first five years of service are approximately four times the casualty rate of the American armed forces fighting at Omaha Beach, Normandy, on D-Day during World War II.

PREVENT THE PREVENTABLE

Sending well means that the sending church participates in and facilitates well-informed prefield preparation to the church's satisfaction before commissioning the missionary. The local church is the best real-life, long-term relational context for personal and ministry maturing. In chapter 10, we described the framework for training the missionary candidate.

The causes of preventable attrition fall into two major categories. Those two primary categories are:

- unrealistic expectations
- lack of relational accountability

The two causes are interrelated: unrealistic expectations reveal insufficient prefield preparation/training (sending), and lack of relational accountability is a consequence of insufficient shepherding while in the field.

The sending church can avoid preventable missionary attrition by applying good sending and shepherding practices. Improving the attrition problem is not the only benefit. Positively, the local church's partnership in a more thorough process of field ministry preparation (sending) and shepherding results in better-qualified and more durable missionaries in the field for the long term.

AVOIDING UNREALISTIC EXPECTATIONS

Unrealistic expectations can only be prevented by having proper and thorough prefield preparation. The well-trained missionary doesn't have unrealistic expectations. They have been guided through training and experience to know what they are getting into. They are aware of the stresses, strains, and pressures of living in the field. The conditions, conflict, and culture in the field will not surprise or cause them to quit.

Missionaries have, all too often, told us with tears in their eyes that they just didn't realize how tough it was going to be, including troublesome relationships in the field. They left the field only one to three years after arrival instead of maintaining a career in the field as they had expected. They needed someone from their sending church to put their arms around them and say, "I know it's tough. You can make it. We're standing here with you. We want you to succeed, be faithful for the long term, and not give up. Do not throw in the towel; do not leave the field."

We received an email from a dear friend who has been a church-planting missionary in a foreign field. Here are his chastening insights:

> For five decades, I have had substantial contact with missionaries from various countries, particularly from the US. I was often amazed by their incoherent approaches, inconsistencies, and inability to comprehend, let alone identify with, the local culture. Many were unsuited to serve as missionaries, either because of their personality, moral quality, spiritual depth, fortitude, or training. Many never went so far as to learn the language. They found themselves in missionary cultural enclaves ministering to one another. The very few converts the Lord granted them were quickly uprooted from their culture and ill-equipped to live out the gospel in the context of their own people. I was also repeatedly surprised by the lack of interest sending churches and the congregants of sending churches showed toward those whom they sent.

This email encapsulates the concerns we are communicating here. Missionaries often lack thorough and proper preparation, including acquiring the language and culture, and local sending churches often do not provide the care and supervision they should. Churches can and should know if their missionaries aren't adjusting or fitting in well. Caring fellow church members can and should walk alongside them so that they can adapt and stay in the field.

AVOIDING LACK OF SHEPHERDING AND ACCOUNTABILITY

The sending church must ensure there is adequate relational accountability. Too often, the missions agency enters the scene after the crisis has grown into an uncontrollable fire. It is terrible. It's almost impossible to heal, repair, and reassemble the pieces once the crisis reaches that level. However, when the sending church has healthy relational accountability with the missionary, the crisis has a better chance of being averted or resolved. Weekly or monthly—regularly—the missionary communicates the nitty-gritty, beneath-the-surface stuff with their sending church. The church is praying for them, shepherding them, and caring for them so that any needs and fissures in the missionary's mindset are known. The sending church shares the need for help with the partner missions agency. The missionary receives counsel, correction, and encouragement to overcome or resolve a burgeoning crisis. Apply the right kind of counseling at the right time. Again, an ounce of prevention is worth a pound of cure.

CONNECT A MENTOR TO THE CANDIDATE

Let's think now about how to bring about a mentor-candidate relationship. It is very significant for the local church or the Missions Team to assign a mentor or a mentor couple for a missionary candidate in training. A mentor is a godly person in the congregation who will learn missions as the missionary candidate also is learning missions. The mentor will come alongside and build routine accountability with the missionary candidate as they go through all the prefield training. The mentor makes time to pray for and with the candidate, meeting with them to discover what is going on in their mind and heart. The mentor asks, "How is it going? What are you studying? What are you learning in ministry skill-building? What do you need help with in this stage of development? How can the church help you in your preparation?"

The sending church and mentor must understand the missionary's individualized plan for prefield training. (See chapter 10 and the resources in the appendices for more information about being/character, knowing/convictions, and doing/competencies qualifications.) Over time, it seems, missions agencies have required less prefield ministry training. Practically speaking, it appears that support-raising capacity ranks higher for them than character, convictions, and competencies. Think about how thoroughly a local church searches, investigates, interviews, and evaluates a candidate for a ministry staff position at the church? The engaged sending church will work hard to ensure their missionary candidate is no less fully and appropriately qualified for their prospective field ministry.

To send well, those directly involved in developing and affirming the missionary candidate's qualifications need to grasp the depth and breadth of the prefield training. The scope of training can be found in more detail in chapter 10. Here is a quick summary:

- Being/character deals with…
    - » the candidate's validation of calling
    - » personal spiritual disciplines
    - » interpersonal relationships
    - » elder- or deacon-like qualifications to go to the field
    - » reputation of integrity in all areas of life
- Knowing/conviction focuses on…
    - » biblical and theological training

- » church planting knowledge
- » global missions and global awareness
- » timeless values of missiology, including principles of indigeneity
- » commitment to lifelong learning

- Doing/competence includes actual, not virtual, life skills, including…
  - » workplace experience
  - » personal financial management
  - » missions field and short-term missions experience
  - » communication and technology
  - » situational awareness, contingency, and personal security
  - » building an advocacy team
  - » language and cultural acquisition capacity

Taking the sender role seriously means the sending church puts its arms around the missionary. Having walked the whole journey with the candidate, the church can say, "We know you. We know your strengths and weaknesses and will help you stay in the field. We can help you work through stresses and bumps along the way. We want to enable you to get to long-term ministry effectiveness and faithfulness."

THE BRIDGE STRUCTURE FOR SENDING AND SHEPHERDING

The Missions Team will want to build a support and accountability team for the church's missionary candidate. Some call this team a Barnabas Team (B-Team), also known as a Prayer and Care Team (PAC Team). It's a focused task force team that may be formed outside the Missions Team. The B-Team is a group of people that specifically want to support the needs and ministry of the particular missionary on a continuing basis. This enabling ministry should include regular meetings. B-Team members should pray for the missionary, correspond routinely with the missionary, and have particular areas of responsibility on behalf of the Missions Team and on behalf of the church. Practically, the B-Team relieves the Missions Team of the day-to-day details, coordinating the care and shepherding of the church body for their sent one.

B-TEAM/PAC TEAM RESPONSIBILITIES

The Barnabas Team or Prayer and Care Team will have a range of responsibilities:

1. Encouragement: The first area of responsibility is encouragement. The B-Team comes alongside the missionary to affirm, assist, and resource them in helping them feel loved and appreciated in their place of service.

2. Logistics: This function includes all the practical concerns of the planning process, such as travel and shipping, along with managing the care and well-being of the missionary's stuff, both at home and abroad. Logistics may also include helping the missionary locate and secure housing, transportation, cell phones, and internet access when on Home Assignment.

3. Communication: This area is a little trickier today due to the extra sensitivities of working in countries classified

as limited or creative access countries. Many countries or hostile regions impose legal restrictions on evangelism or have high security concerns with militants or terrorists. This may involve the B-Team reproducing or managing the communication of the missionary's newsletter, including managing the recipient list. The team and missionary must be careful about how and what they communicate, but they do need to communicate. The B-Team team also coordinates with others in the church to pass along prayer requests, news, and information about the missionary family.

4. Prayer: This is a significant priority in the spiritual life of the missionary. They must be well supported in prayer. The B-Team can ensure that relevant prayer requests are known to the leaders and the church body.

5. Finances: Many finance-related issues are not immediately apparent in the missionary's life: wills, powers of attorney documentation, personal banking and access permissions (even online from a foreign country), multiple financial accounts management authorizations, stateside housing, auto registration, drivers licensing, disposition of personal goods, and so on. All of these are financial concerns. Someone must be available to help the missionary with financial stewardship, including (as needed) planning for their children's education and future needs.

6. Missionary kids: Missionary kids deserve special attention. Their education in the field causes more concern among missionary parents than almost any other issue in contemporary

missions. The rise of homeschooling as a viable option instead of boarding school or cross-cultural mainstreaming strikes fear in the heart of many missionary families. The angst rises with each grade level. Most missionaries never planned to be their children's school teachers. They wonder: Should they ask for a governess or nanny from among their supporters? Do they want to take someone into their home to teach their kids and thus take responsibility for another person in the field? If the wife is doing the teaching, will she still have enough time to acquire the language or languages? What about funding for whatever schooling is chosen? If the option is homeschooling, who can help with selecting and acquiring educational materials? Whatever choice the missionary family makes affects their lives, their ministry, their relationships with their national friends and neighbors, and their kids' futures. The B-Team can hold their hand and help resource the decisions.

7. Security and technology: Missionaries have a heart for ministry. They rarely have training in security and technology. So, the B-Team can fill the gap. The missions agency will often have some rudimentary security and contingency planning training. Implementation frequently falls short. Appropriate personal and home security, situational awareness, and vehicle and technology security might be a project for a short-term missions trip (STM). The B-Team can help with that. Though technology is powerful and valuable, missionaries may lack the skill or impetus to find and install the right things. Sometimes, technology can be

a trap that keeps missionaries from people ministry; this is a familiar snare worldwide. The B-Team, again, can help maintain a balance while using the most fitting technologies to best advance the ministry.

8. Short-term missions trips: Depending on the field access and security issues, the B-Team can manage field visits. STMs can be tailored to the needs of the moment. Certainly, regular shepherding visits by the elders and/or Missions Team are the higher priority. Other assistance or ministry visits should be coordinated and, to some degree, managed by the B-Team.

9. Home Assignment: Of course, the Barnabas or PAC Team will ramp up their activity when the missionary returns for Home Assignment. The missionary will be avalanched with immediate needs related to housing and transportation, phone and internet, health care issues, and personal financial matters as soon as they land. The Barnabas Team can assist them directly when they're at home.

If the sending church sends and shepherds as described above, the church prepares the missionary well for the field. That work, combined with gracious mutual relational accountability, makes the risk of preventable attrition very low. May God give us well-qualified missionaries sent from churches that exhibit a sense of loving ownership in shepherding them well in the field for the glory of God.

HOLDING THE ROPES

The Langfords' Barnabas Team at HBC had a lot of rope-holding to do! Kevin and Melissa were settling into their new situation among their focus UPG group. Everyone rejoiced over many answers to prayers concerning language helpers, housing set-up, and safety needs—plus the wonderful news that a baby Langford was coming!

Still, the Barnabas Team got a report from their regular check-in time with Uncle Vernon and Sara Tennant, the Langfords' mentors, that the move was affecting Kevin and Melissa in unexpected ways. Of course, Melissa's pregnancy came with a range of stressors on her health, her priorities, and the baby's health. Meanwhile, Kevin and Melissa's fellow missionaries working in the adjacent UPG unexpectedly pressured them to adopt ministry practices and a church planting strategy that were very different from what the Langfords had expected. Kevin felt strongly, with sound biblical reasons, that they should stay the course with what they knew fit their plans and methods. All this came with the realization that they had no teammates in their UPG. There was a sense of loneliness and a need for encouragement.

Kevin and Melissa, along with all others concerned, felt that the three-year mark after arrival in the field was an opportune time for them to take a six-month Home Assignment. With the blessing of their field leadership, the understanding of their new neighbors and friends, and the warm invitation of Hopewell Bible Church, Kevin and Melissa prepared to go home for R and R and to deliver their new child.

PART 3

SUSTAINING THE LOCAL CHURCH'S ROLE IN MISSIONS

INTRODUCTION TO PART 3

RETURN TO LOCAL CHURCH MISSIONS PARTNERSHIPS

We've spent considerable time establishing the local church's role in missions from the Word. We've built principles for securing the local church's role in missions on that foundation. Part 3 brings us to examining the specific roles of key players in the global missions enterprise. When everyone in the chain of relationships who is active in the missions process understands and collaborates with the fundamental role given to the local church, the missionaries thus produced will be optimally effective and faithful in the field. We will take a look at each actor in the global missions-sending enterprise, seeing how the pieces fit together to support this understanding.

PREVIEW OF PART 3

In "The Role of the Lead Pastor," we will consider the lead pastor's prime role in leading his church and supporting the development of the concepts involved in being a sending and shepherding church. This involves his role in influencing, encouraging, and educating the church in the work of forming a new direction and supporting structures within the local body.

In "The Role of the Missions Leader," we will see how the missions leader has an expanded role. The leader is not just a committee meeting coordinator but a trainer and mobilizer for the whole church. Functionally, much of the implementation of the strategic focus and the church's part in training and prefield preparation of missionaries comes under this role.

"The Role of the Missionary Mentor" will describe how the mentor of the missionary candidate (and missionary) will be a new category for most churches. It is a very important role in the development and shepherding of your missionaries. This individual (for singles) or couple does not have to be a professional missiologist, a retired missionary, or a pastoral staff member. But they must take their role seriously as the confidant, counselor, and accountability partner of the missionary candidate and missionary.

In "The Role of the Missionary Candidate and Missionary," we will discuss how the missionary candidate or the previously sent-out one may have to revise their concept of the local church's central role in sending and shepherding them. Most missionaries will find this to be uncomfortable new territory. They will learn to humbly submit and give room to the church to enter into their lives in a much larger way than they had anticipated. Yet this new reality will likely become a better source of joy, hope, and encouragement than they could have imagined.

In "The Role of the Missions Agency," we will see how the missions agency must become willing to have a substantive partnership agreement with the local sending church. The biblical priority on the local church can also shape and improve the larger mobilization and recruitment plans of the missions agency. The missions agency that adopts a local-church-centered mindset will discover more blessings and deeper fellowship with sending churches.

"The Role of the Missions Donor" describes how missions donors can learn to be more discerning about the direction of their giving. If missions donors understand the centrality of the local church in God's plan for missions, they will make church planting and church strengthening the deciding priorities for much of their giving. It might mean they turn toward more personnel and missionary development funding and away from major capital projects.

"The Role of the Missionary-Training School" discusses how missionary-training schools will need to adopt and revise their relationships with the churches from which missionary candidate students originate. Doing so will certainly require a higher level of personal engagement with students in coordination with their sending church.

In "The Role of the Missions Mobilizer," we will see how the missions mobilizer can change their orientation from strictly looking for independent individuals interested in missions to discovering churches with candidates or candidates with churches. A significant part of their work will be to ensure candidates are connected with good sending churches that are in turn connected with the best possible resources to help in prefield training and ongoing shepherding.

AN OPPORTUNE TIME

The HBC community was elated to reunite with Kevin and Melissa Langford upon their arrival for Home Assignment. Over the previous weeks, the B-Team had acted on a flurry of back-and-forth communication with the Langfords about their needs and desires for their six-month Home Assignment. This was an opportune time for the congregation to own their responsibilities as a sending church.

When Kevin and Melissa landed, church members met them at the airport with three vans—one full of people who wanted to hug them right away and two with space for all the luggage they brought with them. They were taken to a rented house that would be their home for the duration of their time with HBC. The Langfords broke down in tears as they entered to find food already in the fridge and pantry, every room furnished, and the linens and decor in place. The house was already set up for a newborn. It was amazing!

They were handed keys to their house door and a more-than-adequate vehicle in the driveway. In the kitchen was a notebook of referrals and contact information for everything from medical and prenatal care providers to local stores, auto repair shops, handymen, and counseling services. The church had even solicited special donations to cover the cost of dental check-ups.

The church already had a schedule for a slate of meetings between the Langfords and the B-Team, the Missions Team, and the elders, as well as for a couple of presentations to the congregation. Everyone was excited! Time was also planned for Kevin and Melissa to report back to their partner missions agency, connect with other supporters beyond HBC, and reconnect with family.

Melissa delivered baby Lilias "Lily" Langford on schedule and with minimal complications. Everyone was praising the Lord for lil' Lily. Melissa and Lily were surrounded by loving help and care.

Almost equally amazing was the commitment of another couple from HBC to join Kevin and Melissa in the field. Jim and Liz Elgin entered the missionary-training trail blazed by the Langfords. They became fast friends.

Soon, Kevin, Melissa, and lil' Lily returned to the field. This was their home now. They returned fully supported and were able to purchase a good used car that provided better and safer transportation than the original motorcycle. They began their second term of service with renewed hope and joy.

Then everything just got better. Their faithfulness in language listening and practice, even during their months of Home Assignment, was rewarded by the Lord with serious spiritual conversations. Their neighbors began to ask them about Christ and the gospel. Coming from generations of animism and ancestor worship, they were hungry for freedom from sin, immorality, bondage to familiar spirits, animal sacrifice, and the dark power of shamanism. God gave them new converts! One by one, friends were coming to Christ in repentance and faith. Kevin and Melissa began evangelistic Bible studies with small groups of men and women.

News spread to the church family back at Hopewell. Hundreds of people were rejoicing with them. It was a season of rejoicing in answered prayer.

THE ROLE OF THE LEAD PASTOR

We pray that the Lord will use the concepts explained in previous chapters to build a tidal wave of change in the engagement of local sending churches in missions. Our vision is to see this biblical local-church-centric missiology create more effective long-term missionaries for this last push to reach all the unreached of the world. One worthy result would be much lower attrition rates among missionaries in the field.

The first role we will address is the lead pastor. The position title may be a little different for each church: preaching pastor, teaching pastor, senior pastor, or simply pastor in a smaller church. We're addressing the position that involves the leadership role within the church staff and being the church's primary teacher.

After an intensive weekend of training, orientation, and teaching on the centrality of the local church in missions, one lead pastor said, "This changes the way I think about the rest of my ministry career." This is one small ripple of the tidal wave we're praying for. The real tidal wave would be hundreds and even thousands of pastors understanding the biblical principles and practices and agreeing with that conclusion.

THE LOCAL CHURCH'S BIBLICAL ROLE GIVES THE PASTOR FREEDOM, FOCUS, AND FORTITUDE

Here's what understanding the biblical local-church-centered ministry philosophy, particularly for missions, does for the lead pastor.

First, it gives freedom:

- freedom to not be pulled in a hundred directions
- freedom to minister with confidence in God's design for the local church
- freedom to clearly see the desired goal and outcomes of ministry

It also gives focus:

- focus to choose the best over the good
- focus to invest in discipleship and equipping for the big goal of planting and strengthening local churches
- focus to become more effective because of having a more precise vision

And it gives fortitude, or confident courage:

- fortitude because of a better understanding of the big picture of God's plan
- fortitude because of understanding how the local church engages with and owns its role in missions

Here are typical questions we are asked about implementation:

- What is the role of the senior pastor in applying these principles?

- What is the pastor's relationship to church missionaries?
- What is the pastor's relationship to church missions in general from the pulpit?
- What is the pastor's relationship to the leader of missions in the church?
- How can the pastor prevent the church from getting overwhelmed by missions stuff?
- What priority should missions have in the church?
- How necessary is the lead pastor's leadership of missions in the local church?

Let's describe some examples of how the lead pastor's life and ministry change when they are aligned with this biblical local-church-centered ministry philosophy. These ideas should go a long way to answering the above questions.

1. Walk the talk. Having a robust biblical ecclesiology affects your life. Having a solid biblical ecclesiological and missiology affects your entire outlook on ministry. You are a model for your church family, and you should be engaged, interested, and involved in missions in whatever way you can.

2. Learn the language of missions. Every specialty profession has a lingo or a language that goes with it. Missions vocabulary has its own specialty terms. Lead pastors typically learn a special vocabulary for biblical, theological, and original language studies in seminary. You might find a trusted missions specialist friend to help interpret missions terms.

3. Pray for missions. Make missions a regular topic of your prayers, both in private and in public. Hopefully, you'll move beyond merely praying, "Lord, bless all the missionaries of the world wherever they are, whoever they are." Learn to be more specific about missionary and strategic missions goals as you build relationships with specific missionaries and church ministries.

4. Realize you are a gatekeeper. Who you allow to address the church, who you allow inside, who you allow to influence the people—all of this makes a difference. You want those voices to align with your church doctrine and ministry philosophy in every way. You also want them to embrace this new local-church-centered missions ministry mindset. Learn how to say "no" to sentimental appeals and tangential connections. Reserve your "yes" for the best things. Over the long haul, you and your church will be thankful that you have become a good gatekeeper.

5. Learn to see, teach, and preach missions in the Word. You should see how God's heart for the nations is expressed throughout the Bible. The arc of the storyline of Scripture is clear. God desires to bring glory to Himself in all nations. When you model, talk, pray, and preach in these ways, the result is magnetic; people want to join in with a leader and ministry that are not consumed with themselves.

6. Adopt the perspective that missions is not in competition with your local ministries. Missions is an exponential multiplication of your local ministries. It's not a rival for funds, attention, people, or other resources.

7. Seek to engage the whole church. Pastor, you don't have to do this all yourself. Delegate missions responsibilities to good people. Delegating is part of the role Ephesians 4:12 says Christ gave to church leaders: "to equip the saints for the work of ministry, for building up the body of Christ." Delegation means you allow people to wrap their hands around it, take responsibility for it, and do it on the church's behalf. It means you trust people, but it doesn't mean you never verify that they're doing the right things or challenge them to excel in them. Engage the whole church and delegate.

8. Go, touch, see, feel, taste, and smell missions for yourself. Go on a field visit in which the spotlight is not on you. As a shepherd of your missionaries, be content to shadow your missionary. Learn what their life is really like.

Your influence as the lead pastor is incomparable. No one else can do it. Missions may be limited by your lack of leadership and interest in missions. No one wants the lead pastor to be overwhelmed by doing so many different things. However, you do need to own your influence in order to give it away and delegate things appropriately to other leaders and doers in the church. You're giving them great opportunities and vision for how the Lord may use your local church in His Great Commission.

So, from your unique role in the church, encourage excellence and mobilization through the Missions Team and the missions leader. Speak often about God's glory and the exclusive claims of Jesus Christ and His gospel among all nations. Pray publicly and privately for missionaries and their work. Read select missions materials in balance with your other reading. Ask for help in understanding missions.

Open lines of communication with your supported missionaries and ministries. Every lead pastor should preach a world missions message at least annually. Enthusiastically participate in your church's missions events, whatever those are. Then challenge your people to consider missionary service as a legitimate vocational aspiration.

That same pastor mentioned earlier commented, "Nobody ever taught this in seminary. No class even came close to mentioning or teaching the biblical local-church-centered ministry philosophy for missions." Now that you know and embrace this biblical philosophy of ministry for missions, it will make a difference in how you conduct yourself, your ministry, and your church ministry's end goals. You're the leader, so lead.

ANSWERED PRAYER

It's no secret that all this good news was the Lord's doing. HBC leaders and people felt very weak and dependent upon God's sovereign grace from the very beginning. So much had happened that proved His hand in it all.

Hopewell was now preparing teammates for the Langfords: Jim and Liz Elgin. The church body had learned a lot from their experience the first time. This time, they felt much better prepared. They also knew their missions agency partner better. The questions of who, what, where, when, and why had been answered.

The Missions Team was ready for the Elgins. Jim and Liz were immediately integrated into existing plans for prefield preparation.

The individualized curriculum for their training and experience was charted out. A sequence of rotation for their counsel and character-building was established with the elders. A Barnabas Team was already forming from among the Elgins' closest friends and fellow servants in the church.

The church had matured in so many more ways as well. HBC was the hub of a growing group of regional churches interested in becoming sending churches. Those church's combined areas of focus and experiences formed a strong network of resources for the whole group. There was even talk of creating a support consortium from the church network that would significantly reduce the time needed to raise support. The idea was that missionaries sent from a church in the consortium with doctrine, priorities, and ministry goals similar to those of the Langfords would be able to raise all their needed support from within the consortium.

HBC realized from the experience of training the Langfords that they would benefit from having a similar track for training leaders in the church. Potential church leaders could be tested, trained, and affirmed for leadership in the church, following the model HBC had established with the Langfords. The church was growing. This growth was an opportunity to employ lessons learned to shape and streamline leadership development for the church instead of hoping for leaders to appear mysteriously.

Training became a high-value heart issue for the church leaders.

> # THE ROLE OF THE MISSIONS LEADER

How does the missions leader implement a church-centric missions philosophy? The missions leader's title will differ from church to church. In many churches, the missions leader is a full-time pastoral-level staff member. The title for that position is usually "missions pastor" or something similar. In many other churches, an associate pastor might be the missions leader as one of several roles and responsibilities. Still other churches will have a lay leader or lay elder designated or elected to the role of missions leader. That role might be as chairperson of the Missions Committee or Missions Team. Some have a "missions director." The position may or may not include local outreach. We will focus here on leadership in the local church for global, cross-cultural missions ministries.

If you are the missions leader for your church, you will be helped by the *Missions on Point* podcast. We know several churches that use the podcast episodes as a training tool for all their Missions Team members.

THE MISSIONS LEADER LEADS THE WHOLE CHURCH IN MISSIONS

The missions leader's role is not simply calling the meetings of the Missions Team and chairing or moderating them. The ministry of the Missions Team is not simply making and implementing all the missions decisions on behalf of the church. The missions leader equips and leads the Missions Team to mobilize the whole church for missions. The missions leader has more layers of responsibility in terms of communication, maintaining relationships, and delegating responsibilities to the Missions Team and others outside the team. When the church adopts a local-church-centered view, everyone will be more involved with raising candidates for missions and then mentoring them, guiding them, and tracking them through their development, education, and prefield preparation.

You'll be involved in shepherding these candidates. You are the key person in the church to empower, resource, and facilitate that process. So you may be thinking, "Wait. Help. I need some help doing these things or understanding them." Send up a distress signal! Many resources that didn't exist a decade ago are now available to you. By God's grace, we've seen and been involved in training and mentoring missions pastors and missions leaders in churches scattered around the U.S.

As is the case for the lead pastor, having a well-grounded understanding of a biblical local-church-centered ministry philosophy gives the missions pastor the freedom, focus, and fortitude not to be pulled in a hundred different directions. (See chapter 16, "The Role of the Lead Pastor.")

THE STARTING POINT IS ALWAYS THE BIBLE

To implement this biblical ministry philosophy, one of the first skills you need to nail down as a missions pastor is understanding the church's role in missions biblically. Refresh your study of the Bible's teaching and narrative about the local church in missions. When you have solid convictions, you can communicate and work with your Missions Team to agree on and understand the local church's position and role in God's big plan for missions. Winning the solidarity of your Missions Committee or Missions Team on the church's role is foundational.

Once you leave the starting gate with that biblical foundation, you're off to the races in implementing it for your church. You begin thinking about essentials of the Missions Committee or Missions Team: how it operates, its scope of authority and role within the church, and how to express all of these things on a month-to-month, year-to-year basis. You may want to assess your church in a number of actionable categories of missions ministry. (You can find a church missions profile self-assessment tool at SendForward.org; see appendix B for additional resources.)

You will want to address the challenge of sending missionaries from your church. What does that really mean? How do we identify potential candidates? What, then, do we do with them? (Chapters 10 and 15 can serve as a primer.)

REVIEW YOUR PRESENT STATUS ON ALL FRONTS

You want to evaluate all of your short-term missions opportunities, making them more local-church-centric. Review proposals and plans regarding biblical end goals, other missions goals specific to your church, and the missionaries you support.

Your renewed biblical convictions will drive you to reevaluate the missionaries and ministries you presently support. You, your church leaders, and your Missions Committee have new tools to examine those relationships and the kinds of ministries that you support based on this biblical local-church-centric missions philosophy.

You will want to take steps toward adopting a strategic focus. Doing so will certainly take time and effort to organize. In order to do it well, you will want to include as many missions-oriented members as possible. Then, Lord willing, the church will arrive at an ideal corporate focus or goal for future missions.

It's important to survey and evaluate how your church is shepherding the ministries and missionaries you presently have. This doesn't mean you have to jump on a plane and fly all over the globe starting tomorrow. However, it does mean that you must communicate with your missionaries and discover their needs and concerns. As a function of shepherding care and partnership in ministry, ask them what opportunities there might be for a church leadership, shepherding, or counseling staff member to visit them in the field. The object is not to hijack the missionaries as tour guides or create a road show for the visiting American leader. Rather, this is a special opportunity for a representative of their supporting church to shadow them, learn about their work, experience life in the field, and then report back to the church. The missions visitation is a time to see how the missionary and ministry are doing and try to better help the missionary family flourish for the long term.

GROW YOUR HOME TEAM

As a missions leader, you will initiate starting a Barnabas Team (B-Team) or a Prayer and Care Team (PAC Team) for each of the missionaries most closely aligned in relationship to your church. If they came from your church as sent ones, those missionaries need that kind of core group behind them for support and encouragement.

We have stories of churches and missions leaders that have experienced transformative growth in missions through implementing these biblical church-centric missions principles.

One example is a church in the American Southwest. They wanted to challenge their church with a captivating, visionary focus toward fulfilling the Great Commission. In God's providence, two couples were interested in church planting in an Arab Muslim UPG. The church also had a brand new missions director. Over time, the missions director and the candidate couples alike deepened their commitment through training and consultation. The church was enthusiastic and fully invested in launching their sent ones to the field.

Another church is in the Southeast. The pastor called and said, "Listen, we have a new missions pastor who came from another role in our church. He knows nothing about being a missions pastor. Frankly, our church has a reputation as being 'missions-minded.' But our missions ministry is in disarray. We must figure out how to restart, reboot, and recalibrate our missions to be more local-church-centered in our missiology. We need to have more of the congregation owning and feeling the relationship of the missionaries and ministries we support."

The process of change then began. First, the church elders needed to be on the same page biblically to embrace the local church's role. Then they began to carefully rebuild the missions ministry in the church. They now have a Missions Team that is totally on board with their fresh understanding and responsibilities. The entire church body is permeated with owning and doing missions together for the glory of God.

After several years of taking a pause on an annual missions conference, the church restarted it in line with their values and a biblical local-church-centered missions philosophy. The church is more excited than ever about its missions ministries. The members are having a grand time being involved with and working toward raising, sending out, and shepherding people from their midst to go to far-flung fields for the gospel's sake.

Other churches have experienced a crash course in biblical and practical training in church-centered missions principles. A common response is, "Why haven't we heard this before? We didn't know how to do this. This has been revolutionary to our thinking. We feel that our eyes have been opened. We are so much more able to do and to achieve good things in missions now."

PRESS ON TO THE FINISH LINE

God gets all the glory for many small, medium, and large churches that have opened their eyes to this biblical perspective. They have received the confidence to move forward as a whole church family to own, embrace, and forward the cause of Great Commission ministry because they now understand their role more clearly, biblically, and practically.

Missions leader, may God give you grace and courage to grasp this also. May you grow in understanding and help other leaders in your church to "get it" also. As the Lord gives you encouragement to do so, may you see Him bring more biblically consistent participation by your church. Perhaps you will not feel that you're always swimming against the tide. Rather, you'll rejoice that everyone is with you. You will be that missions leader who has taught, led by example, modeled, and helped them understand their role. Then, by God's grace, a heart for missions will grow a spontaneous wave of outreach within your whole church family, both locally and globally. May it be so for God's glory.

TRAINING BECAME A HIGH-VALUE HEART ISSUE

Ministry exploded for Kevin and Melissa! They were blown away on multiple fronts: a growing interest in the gospel, opportunities to disciple new believers, greater strides in language learning, and the joy of caring for their baby Lily.

Kevin and Melissa realized that they needed to do things well as this movement from God gained momentum. Just as they had experienced patient, godly nurture in their ministry formation, they desired to help these new believers develop spiritual maturity and responsibility. From the very beginning, they wanted to implement indigenous principles. Training others for leadership became a high-value heart issue.

As soon as people became genuine believers, they were taught to identify with Christ in baptism, take responsibility for evangelism, and take the first steps in leading gatherings of believers. The vision was for an indigenous church! So, the Langfords needed to expect their new brothers and sisters in Christ to own it.

Add to this the visit of Jim and Liz Elgin. The Elgins were moving along the training path toward joining them in ministry in their UPG. The Langfords didn't have the benefit of a resident missionary in their UPG prior to arriving. Kevin and Melissa had so much they wanted to convey to the Elgins! This training was continuous and challenging on both ends of the spectrum, from raising new colleagues from home to seeing God raise a new church in the field.

The Elgins' visit was a huge blessing to them all. Jim and Liz caught a vision for the ministry there and for their own future role. They returned to Hopewell with lots of great news and images of God's work among "their" UPG. They even set a target date for arrival in-country. Their return sent a wave of renewed energy through the church body to help the Elgins finish training and to help with support-raising in order to launch them out to the field.

The church was better equipped and informed as a sending church because Jim and Liz Elgin were their second sent ones from HBC. Everyone had clearer, more realistic expectations. The sending church, the missions agency, and the missionaries were truly partners on the same team.

THE ROLE OF THE MISSIONARY MENTOR

The role of mentor we present here will be a new concept to almost everyone. You may hear of a mentor that is a special type of the generic missions mobilizer; that is not what we are considering here. The missionary mentor we propose is a member of the sending church who accepts appointment by the sending church to basically function as a committed prayer and accountability partner for the missionary candidate.

A mentor is a wise and trusted guide, sponsor, counselor, and personal confidant. In our context, a mentor is someone mutually accepted by the church leaders, missionary candidate, and themselves to walk with the candidate through the arduous qualification process to be sent by the local church. A missionary mentor does not have superpowers. He or she simply loves missions and commits to loving the candidate for the sake of Christ and His glory. In highlighting this new role, we describe the mentor in ideal terms. Naturally, we expect the designated mentor to have a good reputation in the church, strength of character, godliness, a good walk with Christ, and a good relationship with the church leaders.

Any candidate finds a mentor helpful. A candidate being sent by their local church has more at stake than one who comes from an outside church. Generally speaking, the qualification standards are higher, and the time is longer. The mentor or mentors must have high character qualifications themselves. They must be willing to open their own life to speak into the candidate's life. The mentor should also be willing to open the Word to help the candidate with teaching, reproof, correction, and training in righteousness.

A WISE AND TRUSTED FRIEND

The local church is the leader and guide for missionary preparation. There is a parallel in preparing church leaders: men who will be elders, members of the leadership team, or church pastors. Often, a church will assign someone to be a prayer partner with a missionary candidate, checking up on them and praying with them. But a mentor is more than that. Mentoring involves accountability and a deeper level of personal counseling and guidance for the missionary's preparation for the field. A mentor is a flesh-and-bones, sympathetic, compassionate, and lovingly confrontational friend who will help the candidate grow as they learn.

A mentor does not have to be someone who is a professional. A mentor does not have to be someone with experience as a missionary. The mentor role doesn't necessarily have to be filled by one individual or couple. It may be a tag-team chain of caring specialists helping with their designated area of mentorship. A mentor does have to be someone who is recognized by church leadership, the Missions Team, and the missions leader as being a godly Christian who loves missions, who is willing to learn a lot about missions alongside the missionary candidate, and who will walk through the missionary's training and preparation for the missions field. The same-gender mentor (for a single missionary candidate) or mentor couple (for a candidate couple) needs to understand the steps involved, so we'll review those here.

MENTORING IS A GAP THAT NEEDS TO BE FILLED

Amazingly, mentorship is a widely neglected aspect of missionary training. In the present day, missions agencies often assign a "coach." However, the missions agency coach is usually focused on accountability for support-raising and checking the boxes outlined by the candidate acceptance process with the missions agency. Missions agency coaches are not typically leader-quality individuals committed to the local church's role in missions or competent to counsel their assigned candidates on character and life issues. Sadly, once the candidate is a member of the missions agency, the agency seems to deem it in its own best interest to get the missionary to the field as quickly as possible.

The local church typically does have qualified people who can be mentors (or a series of mentors). They willingly take a personal interest in the missionary candidate to ensure that the candidate fulfills the expectations to prepare for the field—that is, all the expectations, not just fundraising and checking the box on an assignment.

When we accept the local church's centrality in the whole process of missions, the local church will simplify and shorten the fundraising process significantly. The local church can do that because it gets its entire network of affiliations and relationships interested and involved.

THE MENTOR IS THE
QUALIFICATION FACILITATOR

The local church will oversee the qualification process and ensure the missionary is well qualified, not just minimally qualified. It also should be stated that the local church is not the master of all areas of missionary qualification. Yet the church is responsible for it, like parents are responsible for educating their children. Parents delegate a lot of educational input into their children's lives through whatever school choices, cooperative, or dual enrollment options are available. The missionary mentor and the church may delegate formal and informal training outside the church to cover biblical, theological, linguistic, cultural, and experiential ministry training.

As the missions-sending agency becomes involved, the agency needs to know the lead mentor's name and role. The agency will refer to both the mentor and the candidate for updates on the qualification process. The agency will defer to the mentor and the church regarding qualifications on the list.

COURAGE TO SPEAK THE TRUTH

A mentor ought to have the ability to counsel and guide others. Part of that means the ability to speak the truth in love. A mentor will have occasion to lovingly and patiently counsel or admonish the candidate under their discipleship to move them toward becoming a fully qualified missionary. The mentor must also be available to the missionary candidate for contact throughout their development. The mentor should have the freedom and willingness to ask penetrating questions, listen well, and pray with the candidate throughout this whole process.

Certainly, the missionary candidate's mentor must be interested in other cultures and cross-cultural relationships, even if they don't have specific cross-cultural expertise. They need to have an eager curiosity about aspects of other cultures. They should not be someone who is highly opinionated and nationalistic about American culture and American ideals. The mentor should have a goal in mind for what the missionary candidate will be able to do, know, and become as they approach the finish line of qualification.

Here is a sample list of mentor responsibilities:

- meet with the candidate on a regular schedule
- develop trust and transparency with the candidate
- facilitate evaluation of the candidate's progress in qualifications
- guide the candidate in making and prioritizing decisions about completing prefield preparation goals
- address the candidate's life issues relevant to character qualifications
- encourage and pray regularly with and for the candidate
- initiate, in a timely way, regular conversations with the candidate regarding his or her growth in each relevant area of qualifications required of the candidate by their church and the partner missions agency (see a summary below)
- help the candidate and the church research and identify external training resources that may assist or accelerate the qualification process

DAVID LIVINGSTONE'S STANDARD

The following statement from David Livingstone, a pioneering missionary to interior Africa, was discovered in a missions journal from

1882. When asked about missionary qualifications, here is what Livingstone wrote:

> Missionaries ought to be highly qualified in every respect. Good education, good sense, and good temper are indispensable. A sound mind and a sound body, independence of character, strength of judgment, aptitude both to learn and to teach are of great consequence. An ability to acquire and retain languages, tact in managing others so as to conciliate and yet to retain proper dignity and self-respect are of great importance. There should also be an intrepid spirit of enterprise, decision, cool courage to meet sudden emergencies and to overcome dangers, gentleness, powers of endurance and temperance. We want our best, most able, and greatest men to do the highest and most important of all work, making known Christ's gospel where it has not been hitherto heard.

The mentor should be acquainted with the main areas of qualification, as discussed in chapter 10, "Select Missionaries from Your Midst." There is also a link to a Missionary Training Master Curriculum document in appendix B at the back of this book.

MENTORING WITH A GOAL IN MIND

Consider this summary of training and preparation here in list form. By God's grace, the candidate's qualification will be assisted through mentoring to exhibit these characteristics:

- the *being* or character domain
  - » an internal compulsion

- strong personal spiritual disciplines
- good dynamics in relationships
- the qualifications of a church leader
- integrity in all areas of life
- initiative in and valuing of cross-cultural relationships

- the *knowing* or convictions domain
  - Bible knowledge and comprehension
  - understanding of systematic and biblical theology
  - Bible interpretation
  - missions
  - practical ecclesiology

- the *doing* or competencies domain
  - a broad range of church ministry experience
  - leadership and teaching skills
  - workplace and business experience
  - communication skills
  - ability to use personal organizational tools
  - short-term missions experience and missions field exposure
  - strategic thinking, planning, and goal-setting skills

So, the missionary mentor in the local church plays a vital role. The effectiveness of the mentor can make or break whether or how well and how quickly the candidate qualifies. If, perchance, the candidate mentor disagrees that the candidate is qualified, that could be the gracious providence of God in that candidate's life to redirect or postpone their missionary career aspirations.

Realize that sending missionaries out to the field from the United States to unreached people groups costs a lot of money. The stewardship and the commitments made by people around them and the missionaries themselves are crushed if they have to return from the field too soon or earlier than expected because of a lack of preparation. You may recall that good prefield preparation is the solution to preventing unrealistic expectations, which is one of the main preventable reasons missionaries come back from the field. The missionary mentor has a very significant job. By God's grace, mentors are used in the life of a beginning missionary to enable them to withstand the rigors of life in the field by tracking with them, encouraging them, and challenging them to fully qualify over the long haul for God's glory.

PARTNERS ON THE SAME TEAM

Jim and Liz Elgin arrived in the field! Hopewell and their missions agency partner had a thrilling commissioning service and send-off. It was like the closing ceremony for the Olympics, only much smaller and missions-focused. Hopewell had been praying and working toward sending teammates to join the Langfords. The church could count on the help and support of the sending agency. Everyone was on the same team.

The difference this time was that everyone had more informed expectations. By God's grace, there were now believers in "their" target UPG. A brand new church in the indigenous language was beginning to meet. It was exciting for Hopewell to see the fulfillment of their dream to plant a church among a people group that previously had no resident gospel witness in their language.

NEW GROWTH, NEW RESPONSIBILITIES

The Elgins' Barnabas Team loved them and worked hard to nurture, communicate, and care for them as they started their first language training in the capital city. The Langfords took extra time out of their remote town to help Jim and Liz get settled in.

Kevin now realized that he had another weighty responsibility as an orientation trainer and team leader: shepherding the Elgins through the ups and downs of life and ministry in the field. Hopewell Bible

Church now realized that they had just doubled their commitment to pray, give, care, and shepherd their workers toward the mutual goal of seeing healthy churches planted in the field.

THE ROLE OF THE MISSIONARY CANDIDATE AND MISSIONARY

This chapter is a heart-to-heart talk with the missionary and the missionary candidate. Certainly, the missionary candidate or missionary is at the center stage of missions ministry worldwide. Romans 10 highlights the importance of the sender, the sent messenger, and the proclamation of the message. Romans 10:13–15a, 17 states:

> For "everyone who calls on the name of the Lord will be saved."
>
> How then will they call on him in whom they have not believed? And how are they to believe in him of whom they have never heard? And how are they to hear without someone preaching? And how are they to preach unless they are sent?... So faith comes from hearing, and hearing through the word of Christ.

If you've read the biblical case in part 1, you will know that the local church is at the beginning and the end of missions. The missionary's role is necessary in fulfilling this mandate. This chapter appeals to the missionary to include and help their sending church to take its rightful place in active engagement with the missionary and his ministry. As the church does so, it provides great good to the missionary and the church itself.

WHAT THE CHURCH IS NOT

Both missionary and candidate must realize that the church is not abstract. The church is not merely a convenient resource center. It is not an unpleasant necessity. It is not a human institution. It was not designed just to support you and your missionary aspirations.

WHAT THE CHURCH IS

The church is the local body of Christ in which believers worship, fellowship, pray together, observe the ordinances, and are taught God's Word. The local church is no less than the center of God's plan for maturing and equipping believers to proclaim His glory to all nations. Local churches in every ethnicity are the goal of missions (Matthew 28:18–20; Ephesians 3:20–21). You dare not neglect the role of the local church in your life and ministry. Your relationship with your home or sending church is irreplaceable.

When that healthy relationship exists, it provides wisdom, perseverance, and resources unavailable through any other means. A relationship of accountability between the local church and the missionary is crucial to keeping them in the field.

What specifically keeps missionaries in the field? The first key is having realistic expectations. By this, we mean having proper preparation and qualifications for field ministry. The second is relational accountability with the sending church. Ask yourself, "When something goes wrong in the field, and the missionary comes home, who helps the missionary put the pieces back together and reestablish a life in their home country?" Answer: It is always their home church.

While it is true that the missions agency bears some of the responsibility for the returning missionary's resettlement back home, the extent of their role rarely goes beyond exit and outplacement. If separation from the agency is due to long-term health issues, for example, there is a legal limit of twelve months of organizational responsibility. If departure from field ministry is due to a personal conflict or an issue with sin, the consequence could be immediate severance with no benefits. In the end, the work of restoration, rehabilitation, redirection, or assistance with the transition to retirement always ends up being the responsibility of the home or sending church.

EMBRACE THE CHURCH, GIVE UP YOUR INDEPENDENT RIGHTS

You must encourage your home church to speak into your life, whether you are now in preparation for your field ministry or already in it. Ask your church leaders to get involved early in your preparation and sending process. It's much easier to start now. What if your church doesn't know how to do that? What if your church isn't even aware that they should be doing that? Well, call for some outside help. You should spend time planting seeds of the right kind of biblical understanding of the local church's role so that everyone is on the same page. It may take you extra time to do that. That's OK. It's worth it.

Realize that, as a missionary, you retain no independent personal rights in your relationship with the sending church as it pertains to their ministry through you in the field. Instead, Paul's argument for surrendering personal rights applies (1 Corinthians 9). As a missionary, you will be an authorized representative of your church. You go on their behalf. They are majority stakeholders in your ministry. Christians who sacrificially support you to do specific biblical ministry work also sustain you in the field. You have a stewardship before God and accountability to those donors. Modern Western culture presses missionaries to believe they can live and make choices independently, no matter the effect it might have on the ministry. The question is: How will my personal choices impact the ministry, the acceptance of the gospel, and our fellowship with indigenous believers? The sending church has the right to be included in those choices.

LET'S CONSIDER THE MISSIONARY CANDIDATE

There may be a lot of factors that cause you to believe that you are a missionary candidate. God uses an amazing variety of things to move people toward missionary service. Even though you may feel 100 percent confident that God has called you to be a missionary, you are dependent on people around you, specifically your local church. Your local church is the place where your calling is validated and verified. Having an internal compulsion to pursue missions ministry is right and important. It is equally right and important that the local church has a decisive role in determining whether or not you're fit for cross-cultural missionary ministry. The local church does not allow people to lay hands on themselves.

Only 15 percent of those who say they are called to missions actually make it to the field. If you want to be part of that select group, then you absolutely need your local church's wisdom and oversight. Over a period of time, observation, and experience, the wisdom, collaboration, and ownership of your church leaders in the decisions leading you to the field is invaluable. When everyone is a part of the decision, everyone has some responsibility for it. It will go better for you as you develop as a missionary if you've included them from the very beginning.

GO WITHOUT THE CHURCH?

Can someone get to the field as a missionary without their local church? Yes, it's possible. There are missionaries who love the allure, drama, and prestige associated with travel and international living. Other people pay for their adventures. They may do hard things and communicate well with their donors. Their experiences enrich their life. But this is not an extended college field trip. How selfish is it to do it all for adventurism, even in the name of the Lord, and not have a reciprocal relationship with the body of a sending church? Again, the real question is: How does that unsent missionary presence directly contribute to gospel advancement, planting churches, and training church leaders?

SENT BY THE CHURCH

Missionary candidate, don't go to the field unless you are sent.

Missionary-sending church, don't send a candidate until they are well qualified.

The local church will guide you and help you gain the biblical and theological training you need in the convictions component of your qualifications for the field. They may be able to put you in contact with the right kind of resources for church planting, missions, global awareness, and timeless missiology. Certainly, the whole area of competence—ministry skills and experience—is done under, with, and in the context of the local church. Through that ministry experience, in and with the local church, you will expand your horizons of ministry competence, enabling you to be qualified to do similar things cross-culturally on the missions field. Much of this demonstrates your initiative and diligence to pursue qualifications, study, learn, and apply yourself intensely to prepare for the field.

Don't believe people who tell you that becoming a missionary will be easy. We might oversimplify such promises as resembling this stream of conversation:

Agency Rep: Do you think you're called?

Candidate: Yes!

Agency Rep: Here, fill out this form.

Candidate: OK!

Agency Rep: And get some people that know you to fill out some references for us.

Candidate: OK!

(One to six months pass without significant involvement from the local church.)

Agency Rep: Come to our orientation and do some interviews.

(One to six months pass without the local church's knowledge of the candidate's status.)

Agency Rep: You're accepted! You're a member of our missions agency. Here, do these minimal requirements and raise your support. We'll coach you on how to do that.

(Eight to twenty-four months pass without involvement from the sending church, except for funding.)

New Missionary: Wow! I'm in the field.

Statistically, that simplified system works only if your personal goals are to experience burnout, leave the field much earlier than you think, and then feel terrible about it. Take your time, involve your local church, get them behind you 100 percent, and be well qualified to go to the field. You won't regret it.

CONSIDER THE FIELD MISSIONARY

What if you are a missionary already in the field and didn't have the opportunity to stimulate your sending church to support and shepherd you in these ways? You know you worked hard to get to the field "on your own." Yet you may feel that you're in an emotional vacuum and don't have the prayer support and encouragement you wish you had. You don't have soul care when you go on Home Assignment. You don't expect church members to identify with you well. Everything seems up to you.

Your frustration may stem from not having included your home or sending church from the beginning. You need to have solid relationships with the people who are supposed to be supporting you.

If you got to the field without your sending church playing much of a role, then on what basis will they be able to shepherd you? You've got to help them enter in. You've got to prompt them. You've got to train them, if you will, by guiding, encouraging, and enabling them to enter your life in a fresh, new, and more profound way. Let them know you need them.

They are not just financial prayer partners with you; they should have a sense of ownership. You're doing this on their behalf. You are an ambassador sent out from their local church to do work they can't otherwise do. So adopt a position of humility and need, and let them know that you want them to enter into this missionary work with you. The high road is the low road. Invite them to visit you in the field.

Let them know your concerns and the crises you face in the field. As you foster a deeper channel of communication, transparency, and fellowship with them, you will cultivate a greater sense of ownership and partnership on the part of the church. The next time you go on Home Assignment, it will be very different. People will be asking you questions because you've opened the door for them.

Missionary already in the field, please establish deep roots and relationships with your home sending church.

TEARS AND PRAYERS

When we've described this kind of relationship to field missionaries, there have been tears. They had never known it was even possible. They felt lonely, isolated, and almost cut off from the vibrant fellowship they had enjoyed when they came up in the church and were initially commissioned by the church.

Let's invest prayer in making this happen. Let's tell some trusted friends and confidants within your home church that this is the kind of thing you would love for you, your family, and your ministry to experience.

NOW REALIZING DOUBLE COMMITMENT

It had been about five years since Kevin and Melissa Langford first dropped the bomb on HBC, asking to be sent as missionaries from the church. "I was so naïve back then," Pastor Aaron thought, "and the church was so unprepared. God has done so much! Praise the Lord!"

It was a satisfying feeling. The commitment doubled when Jim and Liz Elgin were sent to the field. The church had also doubled in size in those five years. Hopewell was feeling the pinch in every way, whether it was pastoral responsibilities; space, seating, and parking issues; the spontaneous expansion of evangelism and a missions mindset among the people; or the work of two supportive Barnabas Teams in operation.

It became apparent that Hopewell needed to hire a staff pastor to oversee the growth and development of outreach and missions. Short-term missions projects were springing up aligned with the church's missions goals. The youth seemed to have more interest in pursuing missions ministry. The B-Teams needed some central administrative support. "How We Do Missions at Hopewell" became an annual class and a feature of the orientation of all new members.

The Langfords now had internet available. Bandwidth speeds were slow in comparison to stateside standards. But it was the internet. Better communication was possible. Short videos became part of reports to the church. The latest one featured the recognition of indigenous elders for the rising church. O church, arise!

THE ROLE OF THE MISSIONS AGENCY

Any number of questions arise for the missions agency genuinely interested in the role of the local church. We touched on some of the questions and objections earlier. Here, we want to refresh our mutual values regarding the local church's role and humbly suggest some practical ways to implement them.

LOCAL CHURCHES VALUE MISSIONS AGENCIES

Churches recognize the long history of benefits missions agencies have provided to the church at large. Within the broader church (i.e., the universal church), missions organizations have been inevitable, indispensable, and invaluable to extending missions ministries worldwide. The founding documents of conservative evangelical missions organizations contain phrases like "we exist to serve the church" or "our purpose is to serve churches."

We are especially encouraged to see the trend of missions agencies, both denominational and nondenominational, beginning to open possibilities for local churches to be more active in preparing, sending, and shepherding missionaries. As we've written elsewhere, local churches tend to underestimate the complexities of sending on their own and overestimate their ability to do so. Local churches need missions agencies.

Local churches don't automatically know how to navigate the logistical burdens of sending workers internationally through a maze of legal, political, social, cultural, and business environments. Local churches need the hard-won experience and expertise of missionary-sending agencies. They depend on missions agencies for on-site leadership, guidance, policy structures, safety and security, and a myriad of relational connections for ministry success in the field.

WHAT THE WORD SAYS

A legitimate assumption moving forward is that gospel-loving, Christ-loving, Bible-loving missions agencies understand the biblical case for the role of the local church in missions, a case we articulated in part 1 of this book. If you somehow missed that apologetic, please go back to read and understand it. From the Scripture, we posit the centrality of the local church in missions, and we see gospel proclamation, church planting, and church strengthening as the intended goals of all missions ministry. When those qualities are aligned, there should be no reluctance for the missions agency to improve and grow in local church engagement.

DISTINGUISHING TERMS

Many agencies have added a "church engagement" function to their recruitment or mobilization departments. Some agencies have had a church relations function in their organizational chart for a long time, though it may be inactive. In many cases, church engagement acts externally as promotion and financial development rather than a path for local churches to enter into a partnership for the sake of their sent missionary.

"Partnership" is another term that is frequently used by missions agencies. It's a fuzzy word—both in the sense of "warm and fuzzy" and "imprecise." In many, but not all, cases, partnership means that local churches in the West provide funding and people to the missions agency, hopeful that the agency will accomplish its stated goals. Trust and control are given to the agency. There may be a level of accountability through communication with, or even visitation to, the field. However, the local church has released its stewardship of resources to the organization.

Agency-church "engagement" or "partnership" typically consists of things like the following:

- Local church pastors are invited to an advisory board or candidate introduction and acceptance ceremony.
- Local church pastors or church missions leaders are invited to an agency-sponsored seminar about doing missions better in their church.
- A breakout session at a conference informs the church attendees about the ministries of the agency and how valuable the church's contribution is to the agency's vision.
- Pastors and church missions leaders get on an "insider" newsletter.
- Pastors and church missions influencers are persuaded to bring their congregants on a short-term missions exposure or ministry trip.

- Pastors or church missions influencers are recruited to become advocates for the latest missions agency funding drive.

Yet real church engagement is more than a term describing how the missions organization can build relationships with local churches. It is more than an avenue to recruit more resources for the agency—more than people, pesos, prayer, platform, promotion, and programs.

WHAT IS REAL CHURCH ENGAGEMENT?

By church engagement, we mean that the missionary-sending church takes a prominent role, starting with the prefield preparation and training of the missionary candidate and continuing to the field and beyond. The sending church has decisive input in selecting the partner missions agency and the field for each missionary they send. It establishes a written partnership agreement with the missions agency that defines mutual roles and boundaries. The sending church has a part in affirming their missionary's readiness for placement in a field ministry allocation and may even influence field team strategy and methodology. The sending church also takes a prominent role in their missionary's ongoing care and nurture with the full acknowledgment and approval of the partner missions agency.

SUGGESTIONS FOR IMPLEMENTATION AND DEVELOPMENT

We've given simple answers to some common objections to real church engagement in chapter 8, "Satisfy Objections to Church Engagement in Missions." Now, we'll try to suggest some possible steps toward implementation.

1. Start a church engagement ministry function in your agency if one does not already exist.

2. Learn how to respect and come alongside local churches to help them embrace values and skills related to sending missionaries from their church.

3. Stand up within your organization to defend and advocate for the role of healthy local missionary-sending churches.

4. Change the approach of your recruitment, mobilization, and candidate coaching staff to include developing a meaningful relationship with the sending church.

5. Make way for the sending church to become more involved and own the prefield missionary-training process.

6. Help the sending church develop internal structures for long-term missionary support through a Barnabas Team/Prayer and Care Team.

7. Go to churches that have produced effective, long-term missionaries with your agency in the past and work with them to encourage other candidates from that church.

8. Check your church relationship data to determine which local churches are eager to become a sending church and work with them.

9. Set the tone with potential recruits immediately. Make it a big deal when an applicant sends an application that you find out about their local church. Is their local church ready to step up and take a more significant role in sending and

shepherding them for the long haul? Inform this potential recruit that their call must be validated in the context of their reputation and service in their local church. Missionary applicants need to know right away they will not be allowed to skip over the local church's sending role and become a missionary member of your agency independent of their local church's involvement.

10. When your agency sends reps to a missions conference, #9 applies also. Add "local church affiliation and contact" to every candidate application or interest form, whether physical or digital.

11. Develop a genuine partnership agreement with sending churches, outlining the roles of the sending church, the agency, and the missionary. (See appendix B for links to sample documents.)

WHAT DIFFERENCE WILL IT MAKE?

Doing these things will stretch agency staffing in different ways. Recruitment, mobilization, partnership, and development staff may need meetings dedicated to showing them, first from the Word, the importance of this paradigm shift. As real church engagement grows, the staffing pressure will decline in some areas. The agency will need less supervision of the candidate through preparation, qualification skills, support-raising, and shepherding in the field ("member care") because the sending local church is doing those things.

Doing these things may result in fewer recruits at the beginning. But the quality and tenure of those recruits will be worth it. The logic is that if you have better-qualified missionaries who are better supported in every way going to the field, then the missions agency will have a higher number of effective missionaries who stay long-term. It is a net win for the missions agency.

Let's take a peek at a real example. A good sending church wanted to send a young family with several children to an unreached people group. The whole church got engaged in the context of their love for and fellowship with the family. The couple's B-Team stepped up to help raise their support. The entire church provided ideas for communicating the ministry's vision and contacts. The lead pastor wrote personal letters to pastor friends and the church's affiliated sister churches. The candidate couple shared a joint Google calendar with the B-Team to schedule dates to travel and present the ministry. B-Team volunteers made phone calls, mailed informational packets, and sent emails promoting their dear missionary couple's goal to get out to the field. The Lord used the intense push of the whole church to bring in their full support in record time. And that is just part of what that sending church of about 250 members did to get their sent ones to the field.

There is no question that when local sending churches shepherd their missionaries well, those missionaries don't have high levels of preventable attrition from the field. The best solution for preventable attrition is realistic expectations and a strong accountability relationship with a sending church that owns the care of their missionary as one of their priorities. The governing boards of missions agencies should take note. The current attrition figures should be startling to wise donors. (We gave an overview of the statistics in chapter 15, "Send and Shepherd Your Missionary Well.")

Adopting a biblical local-church-centric model will mean that everyone in the chain of command, from the home office to the field team leader, will have at least a friendly acquaintance with the local sending church's advocate for that particular missionary. The agency will include the sending church in significant decisions about that missionary's ministry, progress, and well-being. A field leader or team leader should expect to get a phone call from a missions leader in a sending church asking, "How is our missionary doing? Is it OK if we visit them this year?"

A PARADIGM SHIFT FOR THE GOOD

For missions agencies, making the above changes may represent a paradigm shift from being more business-oriented and using intermediate growth metrics to being more biblical and embracing quality-oriented outcomes. You may have work to do with major donors and board members to get them to recalibrate their gauges for how to measure success.

The performance goal is not about how many missionaries you recruit. It is about how many well-qualified missionaries you recruit. It's about how faithful your missionary staff teams and ministries are to pursuing genuine biblical outcomes over the long haul. You can present your agency as a servant to sending churches, helping them accomplish their missions vision. At the same time, your missions agency will inevitably make its own reasonable goals and invite local churches to join you in pursuing them. Champion the church's role as they partner with your agency to pursue their missions goals.

Welcome the local church into the sphere of doing missions with you in a genuine, active partnership. Begin to move toward making room for real partnerships with sending churches. You'll be amazed at what God can do in three, five, and ten years. We pray that committing to the proposition of engagement with local sending churches, radical though it may seem, will be a great joy to you as a missions agency.

O CHURCH, ARISE

Hopewell could hardly believe the receptivity of their target people group! It was as if people from that remote language group had been waiting and ready for the gospel to arrive. The Lord had obviously prepared men and women from that people group to break free from their spiritual bondage by gladly embracing repentance and faith in Christ. Delighted, Kevin and Melissa Langford taught and encouraged the group of new believers and their elders to form the first church. O church, arise!

Soon, their colleagues, the Elgins, would join them, begin learning the dialect, and add fuel to the fire. Hopewell was ecstatic. The missions agency was ecstatic. Not only was this an opportunity to share the extraordinary story of what God was doing in the field, but it was also an opportunity to share Hopewell Bible Church's part in everything.

Less than ten years ago, the agency was quite skeptical about a local church entering into a partnership with them. Now, the agency wanted more of the same. They wanted more missionaries who were well trained, prepared, and supported by Hopewell, as well as more local churches copying that intense local-church-centric model. Pastor Aaron and Hopewell had become a spark plug for other churches in the region to observe and learn this new level of local church commitment to sending. Hopewell's influence extended to other missionaries in the field through the gifts of their sent ones as problem-solvers and reconcilers who helped keep good workers in the field for the long term. It all started with Hopewell's commitment to be a sending church.

THE ROLE OF THE MISSIONS DONOR

As we address the role of the missions donor, we understand that this is something that hardly anyone talks about. Communicating with people about how they spend, use, or invest their money is always dangerous. However, Christians should know that the Bible talks a lot about money. The use of money is one of the significant topics of Jesus' teaching. Where your treasure is, there your heart is also.

The missions donor is a missions influencer par excellence, so we offer them the following words of counsel.

A WIDE RANGE OF DONORS

There are many kinds of donors in the missions enterprise. We teach our children to give to outreach and missions. We give directly or through our church to various ministry outreaches and missions causes. There are many appeals for things that seem to be missions because they're helping impoverished foreign kids, supporting disaster or famine relief, or fighting human trafficking. If you give once, you'll soon receive mail ads; appeals also appear in your social media feeds.

Undoubtedly, you are already giving to world missions in some form or fashion through your local church. You have confidence that your church is wise in seeking missions opportunities and relationships consistent with the church's ministry focus.

Many people prefer to give directly to support a missionary they know and care about. That's a good thing. Missionaries deeply appreciate the relationships established with people who support them over decades of missions ministry. Long-term donor faithfulness and consistency enable ministry around the world.

We trust that this book's message will result in donors using their freedom and insight into biblical priorities to focus on the best things to support. Having a clearer focus on kingdom priorities, we believe, will produce the best long-term results for God's glory.

A WIDE RANGE OF OPTIONS

It's a challenge to be a major donor in today's world. So many options sound good, but not all options are equal. There are plenty of appealing presentations in the donor world that are not really biblical missions. Many options are humanitarian without connection to the gospel, much less to an end goal of church planting. It's so easy to become invested in something that initially sounded good but did not have genuine spiritual results. How can we narrow the focus to support the best options? We, as donors, need to ask discerning questions based on sound principles.

START WITH THE GOSPEL

Take a biblical view of the gospel. Don't let others redefine the gospel. The gospel is not giving a cup of water in Jesus' name. The gospel is proclamational in its essence. It communicates the facts of Jesus' life, death on the cross, resurrection, and ascension. The gospel message is woven throughout the Scriptures. From the New Testament perspective, we see more clearly that this gospel message is how God brings people to saving faith. Ensure that the things you give to are rooted in the gospel and gospel proclamation.

HOLD FAST TO THE GREAT COMMISSION

Take the biblical view of the Great Commission. Remember: The Great Commission in Matthew 28 (and other supporting passages) cannot be fulfilled apart from planting indigenous churches. From Matthew 28, we learn that the definition of a local church includes genuine conversion, biblically qualified church leaders, regular teaching of all of God's Word, people worshiping together, and observing the ordinances. The Great Commission is *not* simply evangelism. It is not showing *The Jesus Film*. It is not increasing the tally of "decisions." Making disciples involves evangelism and ongoing discipleship of believers, but fulfilling the Great Commission requires planting local churches. Make sure your giving is related to fulfilling the whole Great Commission, not a disconnected slice of it.

GRASP THE LOCAL CHURCH'S PLACE IN MISSIONS

Local churches are God's instrumental means of getting glory for Himself among all nations. Missions finds its roots in the dynamic ministry of local churches. Biblical missions fruit is generated from the planting and strengthening of indigenous local churches in every nation. Indigenous gatherings of people reading portions of the Bible do not necessarily qualify as local churches unless they exhibit the Great Commission attributes of gospel proclamation, discipleship, qualified leaders, regular teaching of God's Word, and observance of New Testament ordinances. Discriminating questions will discover how the claims of missions appeals align with effective local church engagement on the home side and biblical local church results in the field side. If enough donors inquired and funded based on these biblical markers, missions agencies would change to meet the demand.

TAKE THE LONG VIEW

Try to invest in well-qualified people. Ensure that the kinds of missionaries your generosity supports are representatives of local churches and are equipped to take the gospel and plant churches in other cultures. Invest and be committed to long-term people. Missions is not just a short-term thing. Planting healthy New Testament churches in foreign cultures takes time. Ensure that the agency or organization you're supporting has people qualified to stay in the field.

Long-term investment protection comes through indigeneity. What is the track record of the missions agency in turning over churches and ministries to the nationals? Are they raising up indigenous believers to lead? Are they building an on-ramp for locals to handle leadership well and with integrity?

Invest in the long view of God's glory. As we see God's glory as the overarching theme of Scripture, it unfolds over an extended period of time from creation to the future glorification of the church. Thus, your financial commitment ought to be free of claims of instant results. You're taking the long view of God's glory.

Lastly, invest in relationships. Become personally acquainted with the key players who benefit from the investment of your funds for the kingdom. Know them by name. You may not want them to know you by name. That's OK. Still, it's good to discover the relationships you're investing in and pray they will stay on track spiritually. Ultimately, we all pray that God will give that ministry great spiritual fruit because of your investment.

Your donations can make a difference, not only for the causes you support but also for how it influences the priorities of the recipients. By God's grace, you will grow in discernment and confidence in your stewardship for His glory through the church to all nations.

COMMITMENT TO BE A SENDING CHURCH

In the field, the strategic focus on their UPG was being blessed. Visitors from Hopewell regularly came to check on the work and the workers, the Langfords and the Elgins. Small groups also came to help with the ministry, bringing training materials and participating in outreach and basic teaching through a translator. By God's extraordinary grace and blessing, the fruit of the gospel was spreading to the point where their UPG might even be declassified as "unreached."

The churches they had planted spontaneously asked to be trained to take the gospel to every village in their UPG and to think about taking it to the neighboring UPGs. As a growing multichurch fellowship, they were committed to being a sending church. As a result of consultations with leaders representing the indigenous churches, the missions agency, and Hopewell, plans were drawn to establish a vernacular ministry training center (MTC) for church leaders. It would develop over a few years. The MTC would have modular courses and tracks for a broad range of ministry focuses: youth, children, women, men, worship, and church leaders.

Kevin Langford and Jim Elgin were already training a few key believers to become staff for the MTC. Students would pay for their studies with local produce and a daily provision of labor: cooking and cleaning, gardening, or farming stock animals. Even before there was a simple building, modules were offered, and a handful of adults seeking to train as church leaders arrived with their "tuition," things like bags of rice, beans, potatoes, and chickens.

There were problems and hiccups in the process, to be sure. Local and national laws and permissions needed to be fulfilled. Acquisition of the property with a simple building was not automatic. A short-term missions trip team from Hopewell accelerated the construction process. There was plenty of additional work behind the scenes to make it all possible. Still, it was important to pause, take a deep breath, and express deeply felt prayers of gratitude to God for all He had done.

THE ROLE OF THE MISSIONARY-TRAINING SCHOOL

By missionary-training school (MTS), we are referring to all the training programs specifically intended to provide academic, experiential, and cross-cultural skills development for students training for missions ministry. The category of MTS includes:

- Christian college and university missions programs (including a wide range of international studies and specialty tracks)
- seminary degrees with an emphasis or specialization in missions
- missions-agency-specific prefield training for upcoming missionary candidates
- training for becoming a full-time field leader for short-term trips
- schools with concentrated one- or two-year programs designed for prefield missionary training

- specialized one-to-twelve-week modular missionary trainings for language learning, acculturation, missionary life and work, and missionary team-building
- prefield cross-cultural church planting internships
- prefield preparation for Christian Bible translation, missiology, anthropology, and sociology

In sum, the MTS category includes any training regimen designed to prepare missionaries for full-time, long-term, cross-cultural missions ministry.

ALIGNING WITH THE CENTRAL ROLE OF THE LOCAL CHURCH

Evangelical MTSs don't have any problem agreeing with the biblical centrality of the local church in principle. They readily agree with indigenous church planting as a (if not *the*) desired end of missions ministries. The challenge is implementing a paradigm shift that will give a more prominent role to the local church. Training institutions have to contend with the inertia of existing policies and processes. Change may meet resistance.

Training is a significant component of missionary preparation. The sending church hopes to see their candidate meet prefield qualifications in every area, not just academic convictions. The MTS can be a rich environment for growth in character and competencies.

BUILD A GOOD RELATIONSHIP WITH THE SENDING CHURCH

From the first application of the student missionary candidate, the MTS's database should include contact information for the student's home church. Someone from the admissions or dean's office should find out what the potential sending church expects of their student during or as a result of their course of study. Perhaps the church has good and valid ideas about how the student can pursue character and competencies through extracurricular opportunities.

Maybe the church hasn't a clue; in that case, the school can point to resources to help the sending church. If the MTS wants its students to be effective in the field, it must encourage the sending church in the church's longer-term role and responsibilities. Certainly, while the student is in an MTS context, the home church can and should grow in its ability to be a great sending church. Ideally, you want the sending church to be on track to be the best sending church possible for your graduate.

If the church is aware of its sending role, it may have already appointed a mentor in the church to track the student's development. That person ought to be known to the student's academic advisor.

PERSONALIZED CROSS-CULTURAL OPPORTUNITIES

The school should know the missions student's local church activities and services. Perhaps the MTS has recommendations about churches featuring cross-cultural exposure while the student is in training. The student should be involved in regularly serving in a local church. Growth in local-church ministry skills is part of the competencies qualification grid.

If possible, the MTS should enable opportunities to expose students to experiences that contribute to their target field ministry. Doing so facilitates more personalized discipleship for each student on a cross-cultural missions track.

Simply giving due respect to the sending church's role in the life of the student missionary candidate will go a long way toward more effective training for missions students. This involves a mindset shift more than a program shift. It's about being relational, not being a production line. We believe that acknowledging and partnering with the sending church will result in better-qualified missionaries in the field.

DEEPLY FELT PRAYERS OF GRATITUDE

Hopewell reveled in God's goodness. As the new ministry training center was dedicated in Southeast Asia, the church met to watch the service on live-streamed video. The meeting ended with deeply felt prayers of gratitude led by Pastor Aaron. Also contributing in prayer and reports were key players throughout the process:

- Greg Harrison, Missions Team leader
- Uncle Vernon and Sara Tennant, who were actually on-site in Asia for the celebration
- a representative from the missions agency partner
- Jason Mays, the relatively new missions pastor

The whole church felt a special kinship to this missions ministry because they had all invested so much toward their mutual ministry goal. They were looking forward to further development in "their" UPG and to what God had next for them.

After the spiritual high of that celebration service, Pastor Aaron announced to the church that he would be a part of the selection process to hire a new lead pastor as he transitioned out of that role over the next twelve months and became a semiretired missions speaker wherever the Lord allowed. He considered this church-centric missions effort to be the crowning achievement of his close to forty years with Hopewell. And so it was.

THE ROLE OF THE MISSIONS MOBILIZER

Over the past thirty years or so, "missions mobilization" has grown to be an oft-used term. Stay tuned. Let's consider the missions mobilizer and their role.

MOBILIZERS ARE STRATEGICALLY INFLUENTIAL FOR MISSIONS

Ralph Winter challenged a group of college students by saying, "Suppose I had a thousand college seniors in front of me who asked me where they ought to go to make a maximum contribution to Christ's global cause. What would I tell them? I would tell them to mobilize, all of them."[7]

Phil Parshall, a missionary author and mobilizer, said:

Someone must sound the rallying call. Those who desire to see others trained, prepared, and released to ministry are known as mobilizers. Mobilizers stir other Christians to active concern for

---

[7]. The Traveling Team, "World Christian Habits: Every World Christian a Mobilizer," https://www.thetravelingteam.org/articles/every-world-christian-a-mobilizer.

reaching the world. Mobilizers are essential. To understand the role of mobilizers, think of World War II. As a parallel, only 10% of the American population went to the war. Of those, only 1% [of the American population] were actually on the firing lines. However, for them to be successful in their mission, the entire country had to be mobilized.[8]

Winter is often quoted as saying, "Anyone who can help 100 missionaries to the field is more important than one missionary in the field. In fact, missions mobilization activity is more crucial than field missionary activity."[9]

Fred Markert gives this definition of mobilization: "Mobilization is the process of envisioning and educating God's people about his strategic plans for the world, and it is the means of keeping them involved in moving forward until they find their specific place and role in world evangelization."[10]

MOBILIZATION HITS MAINSTREAM MISSIONS

In today's missions enterprise, many people are called mobilizers or adopt the moniker of mobilizer. Almost every evangelical missions agency now calls their recruitment department "mobilization." It's true. Like in wartime, mobilization is getting the troops to the front. Mobilization is getting all the men and materials needed to fight the

---

8. The Traveling Team, "World Christian Habits: Mobilization," https://www.thetravelingteam.org/articles/mobilization.

9. Steve Shadrach, "How to Find Your Role in the World Christian Movement," Campus Ministry Today, November 18, 2011, https://campusministry.org/article/how-to-find-your-role-in-the-world-christian-movement.

10. Ryan Shaw, "Toward a Biblical Missiology of Mobilization," Mission Frontiers, January-February 2022, https://www.missionfrontiers.org/issue/article/toward-a-biblical-missiology-of-mobilization.

battle on the front lines. It certainly involves missionary training, education, preparation, and logistics.

Often, the people who coordinate or sponsor Perspectives courses (see https://perspectives.org)—whether they do so in churches, missions agency offices, or rented rooms—are called mobilizers. In truth, anyone involved—whether they are associated with a local church, missions agency, or any aspect of missionary training—could call themselves missions mobilizers. They are involved in the whole process of awakening people to the cause of missions. Mobilizers encourage those people to follow God's heart and God's will in being involved in missions for any element of going and sending.

MOBILIZERS ARE MISSING THE LOCAL CHURCH

Missions mobilizers are often involved in discipleship or mentoring people interested in missions to follow the step-by-step process toward finding a field, finding an appropriate missions agency, finding support, and then actually going out to the field. The problem is that most mobilizers have little to no connection with the local church's involvement in, or ownership of, missions. All the definitions of their role seem to leave out the local church. Mobilizers are entirely ad hoc, independent agents, or agents of a missions agency. They don't necessarily understand or foster the role of the local church and its desire to send its people and prepare them well to get out to the field. It's not too much to conclude that mobilizers often short-circuit the process to get missionaries to the field as quickly as possible, whether or not those new missionaries are best prepared for the challenging field out there.

So many missionaries are doing a wide variety of activities they call missions. But many of those activities are not related to the end goal of seeing indigenous local churches planted. Further, those missionaries are not associated with local sending churches that care for them, nurture them, and shepherd them to work faithfully and effectively for the long term. It's no wonder that the attrition rate is terrible.

So, mobilizers themselves must be mobilized to help repatriate world missions back to the local church.

HOW CAN WE FIX THE GAP?

The change required for the mobilizer is similar to what we've written about for the missions agency, the missions donor, and the missionary-training school. That is, change means going back to the local church. If there is someone that you have become aware of, whether you're trying to recruit them into your missions agency or whether you're simply a generic mobilizer that wants to encourage people in their pathway to the field, connect them with their local church. Ensure they understand the importance of the local church for their long-term sustainability in the field. Sure, it's extra work—but you want to be a good and effective missions mobilizer, don't you?

If you're a missions mobilizer in your church, of course, it would be your church to which you're connecting this missionary candidate. The point is to bridge the gap. Do not be a missions mobilizer who simply encourages individuals to do their own thing, find their own mission, and go out there, assuming that God's people will support them somehow.

Bridge the gap so that the local church is a part of the process from the very beginning, from the earliest inklings of desire from the missionary candidate who thinks that God might be calling him to the field. Yes, help provide discipleship for the candidate, encouragement, books to read, websites to visit, videos to watch, and podcasts to listen to. But don't fail to open up the Bible and show them the biblical centrality of the local church in missions. Coach them to develop their ministry in the local church. It is to the shame of the missions enterprise that young, eager adults who want to serve the Lord and give Him glory in the field go to the field with practically zero actual church leadership formation ministry in their toolboxes.

BECOME PART OF THE SOLUTION

Honestly, it's incumbent on the missions mobilizer to study the church, have a good ecclesiology, and understand how the church makes decisions and moves forward. A missions mobilizer has no legitimate excuse for not serving actively as a member of a local church. Use your role to mobilize the church body to accept its role and responsibility in the Great Commission. Not only do you mobilize the individual, but you focus on mobilizing local churches—lots of them. Find the churches that are the most agreeable to being missions mobilizers themselves. Then work with them to help them be the best possible sending church. From those churches, you'll get the best possible missionaries. You'll be part of the solution to fulfilling the Great Commission.

ROLES IN THIS NEW PARADIGM

In the new paradigm that we're trying to describe:

- The lead pastor is the lead missions mobilizer of his church.
- The missions leader is a missions mobilizer for all those interested in missions at whatever level and whatever type of engagement or involvement they may have.

- The missionary mentor is certainly a missions mobilizer for the individuals they're mentoring along the pathway to be fully qualified to go to the field, sent by the local church.

- The missions agency begins to focus more on local churches as the source and seedbed for missionaries. It uses its missions mobilization ministry to help those churches become more and more effective at identifying, raising up, sending, and shepherding their people out to the field.

- Missions donors are asking the right kinds of questions so that they become missions mobilizers, too, using their generous stewardship of resources to enable that to happen.

- The missionary-training school is a missions mobilizer on the training side. Even then, the MTS connects back to the sending local church to enable them to be the best sending church they can be and help prepare the missionary in other ways that an academic institution cannot do on their own.

In a sense, a missions mobilizer can be a blend of other types of mobilizers: encourager, mentor, resource librarian, motivator, and recruiter. They're specific in their intentions, and they have skills. Missions mobilizers need to learn more about local church engagement in missions. Mobilizers would do well to focus more on helping local churches prepare their own missionaries to go to the field. No matter where the missions mobilizer makes initial contact with a potential candidate—at a missions conference, a college campus, a church, a missions-oriented website, or a training program—they need to reconnect that candidate with the candidate's local church. Assure both the candidate and the church that the church's role in preparing and shepherding the candidate for missions is, by far, the most effective long-term factor in this missionary faithfully serving the gospel of Jesus Christ wherever they may go.

Missionaries in the field have tearfully confided that they wish they had that kind of sending church. Today's missing piece in the missions enterprise is restoring the local church's biblical role.

This effort will take patience and grace. It will require all parties involved to learn together. We long to lift up the local church, for which Christ died, to take its rightful place in world missions. By God's grace, we will work and pray together toward that end.

AND SO IT WAS

Hopewell is in good hands. Its members continue to identify and pursue another strategic focus toward fulfillment of the Great Commission. Their solid experience, though it was fraught with everyday human foibles and bureaucracy, now enables them to press on in identifying, training, sending, and shepherding missionaries from their midst. They have confidence in the greatness and purposes of God.

HBC's involvement with the Langfords and Elgins has encouraged other missionary candidates to step forward. Other individuals who want to be sent similarly well have been drawn to the church. Even more, their partner missions agency has asked Hopewell to intentionally influence and coach other local churches to do the same.

Hopewell, after twelve years, has:

- placed three young families from their membership in UPGs
- grown to about one thousand members
- embraced a goal of sending one missionary per hundred members
- had to narrow the focus of their missionary support to only Hopewell members who have served in the church for three to five years
- cultivated a regular stream of potential candidates working their way through the missionary-training pipeline toward full qualification in character, conviction, and competencies
- launched a fellowship of churches intent on doing local-church-centric missions the same way and having the same kind of focus

We now leave Hopewell Bible Church, having peered through the portal of time and space to see the development of a local-church-centered missions philosophy within it. HBC's story is based on a composite of true stories from churches and their journey in missions. By God's grace and the power of the gospel, every element of the story is individually true in history. Stories like this could fill another book. Lord willing, Hopewell's story has inspired you for your church. May God make it so. And so may it be.

CONCLUSION

Thank you, dear reader, for making it to this point. Though we could have spent more time exploring the manifold beauty and priority of the local church, our primary focus has been the local church's role in missions. We have seen both biblically and practically the intersection of ecclesiology and missiology.

We started with the most basic building blocks for understanding "the church" as used in the New Testament, where it is predominantly understood as "local churches." There is no place for missions-mumbling about serving the universal church while effectively excluding local churches. The New Testament is not so confused. Every biblical examination of church and missions functions presses home the centrality of the local church in the life, worship, fellowship, spiritual growth, and ministries of believers. The biblical evidence highlights that the local church is God's plan for His glory and fulfillment of the Great Commission.

The ensuing issue we then took up was: How ought we to adjust our practices to fit the biblical ideal? We put forward seven principles for advancing implementation within the local church. Sharpening our definitions and focus lays the foundations for intentionally pursuing, developing, and sending home-grown missionaries. With deliberate leadership, every church member grows in their involvement in and ownership of missions, including shepherding the church's missionary. The resulting sent one is better trained and cared for than most present missionaries in the field.

In practical terms, how might a biblical church-centric missions ministry philosophy affect the missions enterprise? Everyone who has a part in missions has sound biblical and practical reasons to support a more vital role for the local sending church. We have considered eight roles that, together, frame the whole missionary development and deployment process in Western missions:

- lead pastors
- church missions leaders
- missions mentors
- missionary candidates and field missionaries
- missions agencies
- missions donors
- missionary-training schools
- missions mobilizers

We suggested ideas for practical implementation that cast fresh light on the role of each party in the work of missions. This new paradigm creates genuine partnerships, which, Lord willing, can generate more long-term missionaries faithfully serving in the field.

Pastors and church missions leaders, it's time to lead your church and reclaim the local church's initiative and ownership in missions.

It's time to take responsibility for raising up missionaries for your church's strategic focus. It's time to request and require a written partnership agreement with your chosen missions-sending agency to ensure your church's role in the life of your sent one for the good of the worker and the work. Your congregation will have greater joy and more growth in every aspect of outreach. The biggest winners will be the church and its well-equipped, well-shepherded missionaries.

Missions agencies, it's time for your "church engagement" to grow to enable local churches to become good sending churches. Give unselfish, value-added ministry to local churches. Cultivate them for better-quality harvest workers. It's time to repatriate missionary training and shepherding back to responsible sending churches. It's time for genuine partnership agreements with sending churches that guarantee their ongoing role in the life of their sent ones. The results will be positive in every worthwhile metric: more prayer, stronger finances, reduced attrition, greater longevity in the field, higher effectiveness, and new or renewed focus on indigenous church planting and church-strengthening ministries.

Donors, schools, and mobilizers must apply a more accurate definition of biblical missions and its end goal. It's time to ask discerning questions of candidates and agencies to support the role of the local sending church. It's time to open communication channels and co-labor with local churches to finish the marathon task of the Great Commission well. All of you can influence and enable missions agencies and sending churches to work together for God's glory.

Usually, local churches do not have the experience or means to do everything necessary in modern global missions. Local churches must partner with others. However, the local church must not continue to relinquish its biblical role in missions. It must not cede ownership.

Fully engaged local churches uniquely fuel and focus Great Commission ministry toward its biblical fulfillment.

Who owns world missions? The answer is easy. God owns missions. To what has He delegated responsibility for missions on the earth? Our biblical case is that it is the local church.

People often quote John Piper, who said: "Missions is not the ultimate goal of the church. Worship is. Missions exist because worship doesn't."[11] The ultimate goal pictures heaven. Yet it includes the present and immediate context on this side of heaven. That context is the church. We are not just trying to develop as many independent believers as possible around the earth. We're trying to establish worshiping communities that the Bible recognizes as local churches. That's where the white-hot worship exists now, in our time. Missions exists this side of heaven to establish worshiping communities in local churches in all nations until the task is done.

It's time to recover the local church vision that Oswald J. Smith expressed: "Any church that is not seriously involved in helping fulfill the Great Commission has forfeited its biblical right to exist."[12] Let's pray together that God will enable us to help this change come to pass for His glory.

We hope you find additional resources and answers to questions in the appendices.

---

11. John Piper, *Let the Nations Be Glad! The Supremacy of God in Missions*, 30th anniversary ed. (Grand Rapids, MI: Baker Academic, 2022), 3.

12. James Greene, "Why is the Great Commission Important?," The Keystone Project, July 9, 2023, https://keystoneproject.org/why-is-the-great-commission-important.

APPENDICES

APPENDIX A

WHY IS "MISSIONS" OUR TERM OF CHOICE?

"Missio Dei," "mission," or "missions"? What is the difference between those terms, and does it really matter anyway?

Dear reader, you may disagree, but we believe we ought to clarify our thoughts on these terms and to explain why we prefer "missions." Too much fog clouds our vision about the meaning and use of these terms. We want to be consistent and clear. We use the term "missions" to mean world missions (interchangeable with global missions) and cross-cultural missions, particularly ministry aimed at planting and strengthening indigenous churches.

"MISSIO DEI"

Missio Dei is that grand historic theological term for God's overarching, universal mission and purpose. It includes everything God does, working toward His end goal and objectives for all creation over all time. As such, it is uniquely the work of God. While it includes our actions, God owns and executes His mission. Missio Dei includes so much more than we can possibly do or imagine that it is foolish to think that we can comprehend, much less accomplish, missio Dei. Is it true that God, in His missio Dei, aims to bring universal, comprehensive, eternal glory to Himself? Sure. Do we participate in that through our loving submission to, obedience of, and worship of Him? Yes. Is world missions a vital element and expression of that? Of course.

However, that does not mean that missio Dei is *our* goal or *our* accomplishment in the myriad of good ministry-related things we want to do. People use the term to justify just about anything and everything they want to do. It is far too big, too grand, and too nebulous for us to use as our rationale or goal for world missions concerns. God can use it. We ought not to use it for our endeavors.

"MISSION" AND ITS FAMILY

"Mission" (along with its cousin, "missional") is another ambiguous term we prefer not to use. This is "mission" without the "s," as in "on mission with God," "the church's mission," and "we are a missional church."

Mission is widely used in three ways. First, mission (or "on mission") describes the outreach ministries of the local church within their own community. Second, mission can denote all kinds of ministries outside the church, including world missions. Third, in a more secular and generic sense, mission refers to a specific target goal or assignment.

The main problem is that using mission for ministry related to the church in these ways requires additional clarification. It is too generic and nonspecific. Most of the time, when a "missional" church talks about mission, it refers to local ministries, rarely to world missions. In an expression popularized by Henry Blackaby, every Christian should be "on mission with God." Churches that emphasize the term "mission" often believe that world missions is a distraction from their mission or "being on mission." They tend to feel that world missions competes for people and resources with their primary goal of expanding their church's statistical reach. This mindset comes from the secular idea that corporate resources are a zero-sum game. It entails resource competition, polarization, and a silo mentality. It looks at church resources as limited, so that if one area of ministry gets a bigger piece of the pie, all other ministries get smaller slices. Thus, missions detracts from their mission. In the world of church growth or church planting, measuring outcomes may have more to do with numbers and tangible results than with spiritual depth and a balance of ministry, including ownership of and participation in world missions. We tend not to give much world missions credit to church leaders who reflexively state that their church does "mission" or is "missional." These catchwords are all show and (sometimes literally) smoke and mirrors.

"MISSIONS"

Let's stop using nebulous, ambiguous, or distracting terms. "World missions," "global missions," or simply "missions" (with the "s") traditionally and accurately means cross-cultural outreach beyond the natural geographic reach of the church body. That's the way we use the term "missions" here. We argue in this book that missions should prioritize an intentional connection to pioneering the planting of indigenous local churches or, by extension, strengthening existing national churches to do the same. Using the term "missions" this way clarifies what we mean.

Using missions in this way also stands in contrast to cross-cultural humanitarian efforts, including community development, disaster relief, human trafficking prevention, social justice work, sports ministry, well drilling, building projects, and educational advancement. These good ministries are not, in and of themselves, missions. These kinds of activities may be a tactical means to missions when they include the intentional verbal proclamation of the gospel and link that work to planting or strengthening indigenous local churches. They may be termed "ministry" in the sense of serving others. Those ministries may be temporally significant to the recipients, even life-saving or elevating. They can be noble, sacrificial, and deserving of praise. Apart from the intentional verbal proclamation of the gospel, however, they are not salvific in content. They are not eternal. They are not world missions in a biblical sense, at least not in the way we understand and use the term.

Many church-sponsored and parachurch ministries are going into the world doing good and valid things for needy people. However, it doesn't seem accurate to call their work biblical missions unless they are contributing to the goal of proclaiming the gospel and bringing those disciples together into mutually committed bodies of believers who worship our Lord Jesus Christ.

A healthy missions mindset doesn't think of missions as a competitor for resources among other ministries. Rather, it sees missions as the center and reason for the church's existence! A biblical missions mindset understands that God's resources are not limited by our own. Missions fuels and informs every ministry of the church. God's relentless purpose is to see His glory exalted in all nations. He has appointed and commanded us to be His agents to accomplish this very thing. So many pastors and church leaders have discovered that when their local church gets missions right, God blesses and supplies everything else in the church.

Using the term "missions" in this way will help us clear the fog and be more consistent.

APPENDIX B

WHAT ARE GOOD RESOURCES FOR CHURCH MISSIONS DEVELOPMENT?

It's been my privilege, by God's grace, to work with key organizations focused on local church missions mobilization:

- ACMC (ten years), originally known as Association of Church Missions Committees and, later, as Advancing Churches in Missions Commitment, until its dissolution in 2004. ACMC developed a reputation for excellence in local church missions administration, printed resources, and missions leadership training through conferences.

- Propempo International (twenty years), from 2003 to 2023, as founder and General Director. Propempo International was formed to assist development of biblical local-church-centered ministry. Hundreds of articles, blogs, podcasts, media, and printable resources are its legacy. Create your own PDF booklet from Propempo materials online.

- Presently, Propempo merged (as of 2023) as a subsidiary with MissioSERVE Alliance. MissioSERVE's vision is "to lead the way in aligning the sending church and missionary to accomplish their mission together." MissioSERVE has become one of a brave vanguard of missions-sending agencies committed to honor and partner with the local church's biblical role in equipping, sending, and shepherding missionaries.

- Send Forward is a newer organization aimed at creating and curating resources available through its website for biblical local-church-centered global missions ministry. We help local churches send well-qualified missionaries for long-term service to the neediest fields of the world. We provide individualized training for local churches, missions-sending agencies, and missionaries through our partner organizations Propempo International and MissioSERVE Alliance.

- You can learn more and contact key people through:
  » https://missioserve.org; https://missioserve.org/contact
  » Career missionary training: https://missioserve.org/go/career-missions
  » https://propempo.com; ministry@propempo.com
  » https://sendforward.org; info@sendforward.org

CHURCH MISSIONS TRAINING AND DIAGNOSTICS

1. **Sending Church Readiness Inventory** [https://bit.ly/ChurchReadiness]. The Readiness Inventory lets the MissioSERVE church engagement staff see a snapshot

What Are Good Resources for Church Missions Development?

of your church's present missions values, framework, and commitments with a view to assisting your church in becoming a great missions-sending church.

2. **Church Missions Profile** [https://sendforward.org/store]. The CMP is a self-assessment profile of your church's performance vs. standardized benchmarks of top churches in twelve areas of missions ministry. The assessment results in an individualized report of approximately fifteen pages, giving you specific ideas and resources to improve your score in every area. Depending on the version, your assessment input can come from one person or up to ten persons:

   » Individual input CMP [https://bit.ly/CMP-one-input]

   » 10-person input CMP [https://bit.ly/CMP-10user-input]

3. *Missions on Point* **podcast episodes** [https://propempo.com/resources/missions-on-point-podcast]. The *Missions on Point* podcast is available on most major podcast apps. Each episode lasts about fifteen minutes, and a new episode is released every Friday. Topics cover a wide range of issues related to church missions, missiology, biblical missions, missionary life, and missions preparation. No blather, no banter, just good content. The podcast espouses a local-church-centered philosophy of missions we call "the Propempo perspective on church and missions." There are presently four years of weekly topics available.

4. **Church Partnership Agreement Template** [https://sendforward.org/store/church-partnership-agreement-template]. This template is offered as a means for your church

to partner with MissioSERVE Alliance and to agree on the cooperative roles in sending your missionary to the field. Our biblical convictions place the final authority for the work and well-being of the missionary on the local sending church. MissioSERVE informs, engages, and enables the local church and the missionary in their responsibilities. We also provide field- and home-side developmental resources, based on our experience, to benefit the church and ministry. Contact Propempo church engagement staff for personalized solutions.

5. **MissioSERVE's Church-Centric Missions Process: Evaluation, Education, Elevation** [https://sendforward.org/store/church-missions-development-questionnaire]. Global missions coaches use this preliminary questionnaire to provide churches with individualized tools and advice that will enable them to create a robust, church-centered, biblical missions strategy. Ideally, this process will involve church leaders, the Missions Team, and interested members. This church engagement process typically transpires over three phases: evaluation, education, and elevation.

6. **The Sending Church VISION: Training.** The VISION process is an example of the educational component of MissioSERVE's church engagement. We walk through each step, alliterated as "V-I-S-I-O-N," teaching and giving examples of a local church's Values, Identity, Strategy, Implementation, Ownership, and Nurturing. The local church is equipped to build and implement the mindset of a sending church.

7. **The Institute for Church-Centered Missions.** Be on the lookout for this exciting new partnership between Reaching & Teaching and 9Marks. Cohort-style learning opportunities are available for global workers, sending church pastors, church members, and aspiring missionaries.

MISSIONARY-TRAINING CURRICULUM

1. **Missionary Training Master Curriculum** [https://sendforward.org/store/missionary-training-master-curriculum]. This is a model of a complete potential training and preparation curriculum for any missionary to any people group in a brief outline form. It is comprehensive and intended to be customized in order to provide the most appropriate and needed training and experience for each person and each target ministry. The training curriculum assumes that formal education, structured ministry experiences, and specialized or technical external training will complement the less formal character development and relational discipleship that is nurtured in the candidate's home church. It includes the three major areas of concern:

   » character (alternately, *being* or heart)
   » conviction (alternately, *knowing* or head)
   » competence (alternately, *doing* or hands)

2. **MissioSERVE's D3 Missionary Training Process** [https://missioserve.org/go/career-missions]

OTHER RESOURCES

1. **Missions funding.** Although we did not address church-centered missions funding in detail, here are two resources to get you started on that thinking:

    a. A Missions Funding series of podcast on Missions on Point beginning with episode 69.

    b. An article on Propempo.com titled "How is missions funded at our church?"

2. **Online Training**

    a. SendForward.org: Short video-based course for Missions Teams. [https://sendforward.teachable.com/p/missions-101]

    b. Missions Path PDFs: See Propempo.com to create your own PDF booklet of articles you can select from among the hundreds available. [https://bit.ly/your-PDF]

    c. See Propempo.com to create solutions for your church using SendForwardAI. [https://bit.ly/SendForwardAI]

    d. The Greenhouse: An online resource made available by Pioneers. [https://pioneers.org/greenhouse]

    e. Biblical Ministries Worldwide has a great series called "Senders Videos." Forty-one videos with three-minute answers to questions about being a sending church. [https://vimeo.com/showcase/6247560]

3. **Missio Nexus**, a large and broad association of churches and organizations, has a full-time church engagement director. [https://missionexus.org]

4. The organization **Sixteen:Fifteen** provides church missions coaching and resources for Great Commission work. [https://1615.org]

5. The organization **9Marks**, among other things, spends a good deal of time equipping the church to obey the Great Commission. [https://www.9marks.org]

6. **Radius International** provides prefield missions training, and they've got a good ecclesiology. [https://radiusinternational.org]

7. **Upstream Collective** is a resourcing ministry, and Upstream Sending is the associated sending arm. [https://www.theupstreamcollective.org] [https://www.upstreamsending.com]

8. **Church associations**

    a. FIRE: The Fellowship of Independent Reformed Evangelicals [https://www.firefellowship.org]

    b. RBnet: The Reformed Baptist Network [https://reformedbaptistnetwork.com]

    c. ACME: Association of Churches for Missions and Evangelism [https://acmefellowship.org]

9. **Church planting networks:** Acts 29, Pillar Network, Treasuring Christ Together, Harbor Network, Send, Redeemer City to City, Converge, and many more!

APPENDIX C

HOW DO WE CHOOSE A MISSIONS AGENCY PARTNER?

How do we choose a missions agency partner? What criteria should we use to select one for our strategic focus?

These questions are frequently asked by churches seeking a partner in their missions initiative. We'll submit thoughts in this appendix to help you narrow the options.

Everything about the sending church and its target ministry informs the decision. Even when a church asks all the right questions of all the right missions agencies, the final answer may not be a perfect fit. A near-perfect fit for one field or focus may not be the same best fit for every target ministry and field.

CURRENT AGENCY RELATIONSHIPS ARE A POSSIBILITY

Before exploring further, do an inventory of your current agency relationships.

1. If your church is denominational or is affiliated with other like-minded churches, add that connection to your possibilities.

2. The denominational missions agency or affiliation-approved partner may or may not be ideal for your specific opportunity.

3. Denominational agencies may not have the same biblical convictions, priorities, or focused goals as your church. Their costs may be unacceptably high.

4. Don't accept your denominational outlet as the best fit without asking questions specific to your intended field ministry and strategic focus.

5. It's OK to require a partnership agreement to protect your church's role and missionary's shepherding care.

6. Some churches today have narrowed their sent ones going with their denominational agency to a short list of acceptable field ministry teams that match their church's values, methodologies, and ongoing role in shepherding.

7. Ask questions of the missions agencies through which you already support missionaries who are focused on similar biblical priorities. Ask them if they are willing to sign a partnership agreement with your church in order to pursue your specific missions vision or focus. Then dig deeper. Ask questions about how they see such an agreement giving your church a central role in the qualification, life, ministry, and outcomes of your sent one.

CHECK WITH CURRENT MISSIONARIES OR HISTORIC CONNECTIONS

Does your church presently support work or have a history of support for ministry in the country of your chosen strategic focus?

1. Ask the missionaries and ministries you presently support to give you suggestions about missions agencies that fit your vision goals. They probably have some field intelligence about agencies with a good reputation. Their information and guidance might save you a lot of time and effort.

2. The leaders or your missionary candidate could be assigned to do a little historical research into missions outreach in the area of your target focus. There is a good probability that someone or some group has had some contact, intentions, or prior ministry experience in that place or people group.

CLARIFY FOUNDATIONAL DOCTRINAL CONCERNS

You should have fundamental concerns based on your church's doctrine and missiological implications. Here are some things to ask and consider:

1. Does the agency understand the gospel? What is their definition of the gospel? Do they believe and practice the priority of biblical proclamation of the gospel? You might be surprised that some well-known missions have allowed their missionaries to adopt a "presence evangelism" stance. This was the practice of liberal modernism a lifetime ago. Now, it has made its way into otherwise conservative missions agencies. Beware. Ask questions.

2. What is the agency's definition of a believer? How does a person become a New Testament Christian? Again, don't be surprised by some common reinterpretations of a biblical answer. An individual becomes a believer through repentance and faith in Jesus. Historic Reformation truths apply: by grace alone, through faith alone, in Christ alone. A New Testament believer doesn't simply attend meetings and obey a legalistic formula.

3. What is the agency's definition of a local church? It's hard to believe that Western missions have declined to the level of not having a sure and sound answer to this question. The agency might self-disqualify if they ask in reply, "What do you mean by that?" What does it take to be a church in New Testament terms? This question is very important if indigenous church planting and strengthening is the primary goal!

4. How does a new believer qualify to become a church leader? This seems like a simple question, but it's not. If you are from a strict denominational church community, the answer might be formalized as an arduous training process toward ordination in the denomination. If you are from a more autonomous church, your qualification for church leadership might be informal. The Bible is clear about the qualifications for church leaders, but it is less clear about the process. Again, if your church's focus is to plant and strengthen indigenous local churches, this becomes an important question to settle before your missionary gets caught in the crosshairs of controversy in the field.

5. Ministry methodologies are often tied to doctrine-related issues. Some missions agencies have a required curriculum and methodology. You should know about this before proceeding. Others have one primary set of methods, means, or tools they virtually require of their missionaries and field teams. Take time to review and understand what they use or promote.

We've seen many field teams torn apart and workers wounded by fiery disagreements on the issues addressed in this section. Try to ascertain, as much as possible, that your missionary will be placed in a team that agrees with your church on the fundamentals. Your church-agency partnership agreement should provide latitude for your church to ensure your sent one does not become a negative attrition statistic due to incompatibility with the team to which they are assigned.

COUNT THE FINANCIAL COSTS

This may seem like a secondary issue, but the assessment of funds received to support your missionary can be a source of discontentment. Let's count the cost before building that tower. Remember that you are essentially paying for services. If you had to provide everything for your missionary directly as a church—including the value of your volunteer or staff labor—the costs would probably be higher than going through a missions agency.

1. If you send your missionary through a denominational agency, maybe you never see the costs; but they are there. It can be discouraging to discover that funds donated for your missionary's livelihood in the field are spent on sustaining a large bureaucracy.

2. Orientation and training expenses are either built into the support quota or accessed cafeteria-style; you pay for what you get. A candidate orientation itself can cost a couple of thousand dollars per adult, with additional costs for children. Specialized trainings in such areas as Bible and theology, linguistics, language, first aid, and security come with a cost.

3. Every missions agency builds in certain amounts or percentages for overhead costs. Most admin expenses are necessary services like accounting, donation records and receipting, legal reporting, insurance, and retirement plans.

4. There are a number of other common costs which take their toll.

    a. Field (in-country) services like immigration, procurement of legal documents, field management, and daily administration work.

    b. Field or regional missionary conferences and retreats. They may not be held annually, but these obligatory meetings require the missionary to set aside funds to cover the costs of those gatherings, whether the missionary attends or not.

    c. In some cases, the local field team may assess a certain amount to cover the team leader's admin expenses and certain joint team expenses for special meetings, materials, etc.

5. Ask questions and avoid problems before signing papers committing your church and missionary to a particular missions agency.

a. Will your church be able to insist on an appropriate level of language proficiency before your missionary is released from "full-time" language study?

b. Will your church be free to know and interact with whatever methodologies your missionary and their assigned team choose for evangelism, discipleship, and church planting?

c. How will believers be trained for leadership within the growing body of Christ?

d. How is a church plant recognized as an organized church in the culture and region of the field ministry?

e. Is there a church fellowship, association, affiliation, or denomination that the new church plant is expected to join?

f. What are the criteria for your missionary moving to another team or community for planting another church?

g. What options or resources are there locally for educating our missionary children?

APPENDIX D

IS MY CHURCH TOO SMALL?

Most churches consider themselves to be small churches. Statistically, 92 percent of churches have an average attendance of less than 250.[13] In our experience, smaller churches tend to feel that they don't have the bandwidth or resources to implement the principles taught in this book. Many are skeptical of ever being able to be a strategically focused, missionary-sending church. As a church leader, you may be one who thinks:

- "My church is too small."
- "We are a relatively new church plant."
- "We are too rural to have the resources to do this."
- "We're just a house church."

---

13. "Now, 2 in 3 U.S. Protestant churches (68%) have congregations of fewer than 100 people, including 31% who have fewer than 50. A quarter of churches (24%) fall into the 100-249 range, while 8% of congregations host 250 or more each week." Aaron Earls, "Churches Are Open but Still Recovering from Pandemic Attendance Losses," Lifeway Research, November 8, 2022, https://research.lifeway.com/2022/11/08/churches-are-open-but-still-recovering-from-pandemic-attendance-losses.

- "Our pastor is bivocational because we can't afford to support him fully, much less give significant support to send one of our own as a missionary."
- "Let's keep doing what we are doing, supporting a few missionaries we know. Later, when we're bigger, we'll shift toward being a sending church."

The well of human resources, finances, and expertise seems shallow. Everyone would agree with this evaluation... until there is a Kevin and Melissa Langford moment, like in the Hopewell Bible Church story, when a young couple steps up and says, "We think God is calling us to be missionaries. We'd like our church to be our sending church." At that point, hearts melt. Resistance turns into receptivity.

TRUST GOD AND TAKE THE FIRST STEP

Church leader, if you think you can't become a sending church, that thought will become a self-fulfilling prophecy. However, through faith and prayer, we've seen smaller churches succeed when they lean into the ideal goal of becoming a local sending church. It starts with embracing the Bible's message of the centrality and significance of the local church in His plan. Then the local church intentionally elevates missions involvement as an aspiration for their people. Teaching and exposing your church to the concept of God's glory on display in the local church also reinforces the members' commitment to their church.

TAKE THE LONG VIEW

Commit to the goal of becoming a missions-sending church. Take some simple steps toward that goal:

1. Evaluate your present missions commitments and align them with your church values and the principles learned in this book. That is, support only those missionaries and ministries:

    a. with whom you can have a sustained personal relationship

    b. who focus on gospel proclamation and biblical missions goals

    c. who facilitate your church having a sense of ownership and participatory partnership in their ministry

2. Reach out to like-minded churches in your area or region that are similarly committed to your missions ideals. Perhaps a missionary candidate from one of your "missions consortium" churches will be the first sent one from among those churches.

3. Find a way to give your congregation more missions exposure through a few of them going on a field visit, a vision trip to a field (not a tourist trip), or a missionary care-shepherding trip.

4. Put out inquiries to learn from other small churches further down the path of church-centric missions sending. Adapt what you discover from them to your situation.

5. Empower and delegate ongoing missions education and communication to responsible missions lovers in your congregation.

PRAY THAT GOD GRANTS YOU A MISSIONARY CANDIDATE

Ideally, a candidate arises from among your congregation. However, other possibilities might be:

- a pastoral intern who turns into a beloved candidate "from" your congregation
- a new family that joins the church and has a young-adult child with dreams of being a missionary someday
- someone studying for missions ministry in a nearby Christian training school who makes your church their home church, at least for their student years

Missions insights gained as you teach through God's Word have a long-term effect on the dreams and heartstrings of your people. Over time, God uses your priorities and passions to light a fire of commitment.

GIVE GOD THE GLORY WHEN IT HAPPENS

While it is true that your resources are limited, it is incredible what resources show up when the need arises. Local resources may be small, but God is so much bigger than we imagine. Below are a few true anecdotes we are pleased to share about small churches that have walked this path before you.

SMALL CHURCHES, BIG BLESSINGS

1. A small church in North Atlanta, Georgia, had a vision to provide gospel ministry to the refugees and disenfranchised from the war in Bosnia. By God's grace, "coincidences"

came together. Within a few years, nearly everyone over age fifteen in their church had ministered in the displaced persons camps there. Resident missionaries counted more conversions to Christ among Muslims in that handful of years than in the previous fifty years in the region. Read about it in John Rowell's book, *Magnify Your Vision for the Small Church* (Atlanta: Northside Community Church, 1998).

2. A small urban church plant in Montgomery, Alabama, learned and became committed to the principles in this book. They were praying for opportunities. The Lord provided. Here's an excerpt from an email dated March 2015:

> Our church's vision for missions is about to explode! We challenged our church to spend one week of 2015 in a cross-cultural missions context!… The Lord has blessed it mightily!!! We just commissioned nine people from our church to go to Ecuador for a week!! They leave Saturday!!!
>
> We have 3 [or] 4 people signed up to go to Kenya in July. We have five signed up to go to Clarkston, GA, in June. [Clarkston is the most ethnically diverse square mile in the U.S.] We have 2 going to Thailand in June. One is going to Nigeria in August. There are only 38 adults in our congregation, LOL!!!

3. A tiny church on an island in the Chesapeake Bay is very committed to church-centered missions. They haven't had a paid pastor for fifty years. Yet God has used them to send

half a dozen missionaries over the years. They also faithfully and strategically support at least a dozen others.

4. A small church in Southern California became the sending church for their pastor's family to go to an unreached people group in the Muslim world.

5. A small church in Virginia committed to forming a multicultural team along with graduates from a Bible school they supported in Mexico. The goal of the team was to plant churches in the Middle East.

6. A small church in New Hampshire raised and steadily helped one of their own families become qualified and sent as missionaries in the Balkan region.

Small sending churches tend to serve more, give more, and send more missionaries per capita than large churches. No, your church is not too small.

MissioSERVE seeks to lead the way in aligning the sending church and missionary to accomplish their mission together.

HTTPS://MISSIOSERVE.ORG/

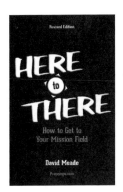

What happens after you feel God's call to missions? How can you move along the path from initial commitment HERE to actual arrival THERE in missionary service? More than 8 out of 10 missionary candidates fail to get to the field. Many intend to go; few make it.

https://sendforward.org/store/here-to-there-how-to-get-to-your-mission-field-revised-edition-pdf/

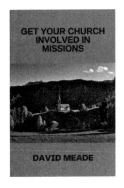

Aimed at evangelical church leaders, Get Your Church Involved in Missions provides biblical and practical motivation for local churches to take the initiative in restoring the rightful place of the local church in missions and missions in the local church.

https://sendforward.org/store/get-your-church-involved-in-missions-pdf/